THE DON'T SWEAT GUIDE
FOR MOMS

Other books by the editors of Don't Sweat Press

THE DON'T SWEAT GUIDE
FOR MOMS

Being More Relaxed and
Peaceful So Your Kids Are, Too

By the Editors of Don't Sweat Press
Foreword by Kristine Carlson

New York

ISBN 0-7868-8727-3

FIRST EDITION

10 9 8 7 6 5 4 3 2 1

Contents

Foreword

Like most moms, being one is the most important part of my life. Above anything else we do as women, we definitely make a contribution to the world through our children. While motherhood is by far the most rewarding job of all, it is not without daily challenges. Much of the time, we feel overworked and under-appreciated, yet we take enormous pride and joy in our children. I've never met a mom who would trade the gift of being a mother for anything else.

Where would we be without moms? I'm ever grateful to my own mother for bringing me into this world and for giving so much of herself. I certainly didn't give her the appreciation that she deserved while I was growing up, but all that has changed since becoming a mother myself. Every day, I thank my lucky stars that I have such a great mom!

Every mother has experienced the joy along with the stress that comes with the territory. Some of the challenges we face are unique, but many are universal.

We are fortunate to live in a world where help comes in many forms. The editors of Don't Sweat Press have done a fine job in creating a guide to help take some of the stress out of mothering.

I have found that you can't receive enough inspiration in raising children. Whether you're feeling swamped, rushed, a bit too busy, or you just need some good ideas, this book will assist you. It's written in a friendly, unthreatening tone, and the advice is pretty darned good!

Sometimes we over-commit or have too many things going on. Other times, we blow things out of proportion or overreact. Or we try too hard to be perfect, or we overanalyze an issue with our kids. In other words, we use our thinking in ways that take us away from the joys of parenting. Instead of relying on calm wisdom and common sense, we engage in habitual reactions and habits that contribute to further stress.

The Don't Sweat Guide for Moms was written to address the fact that at least some of the stress and frustration we experience is self-created. In other words, there are subtle (and sometimes not-so-subtle) ways that we make things harder than they need to be. I'm the first to admit that we all fall into this trap from time to time.

Please join me in thanking all mothers for making life on this planet possible. I also want to thank you for being the best mom you know how to be, and especially for being willing to continue to grow and learn. I hope this book is of tremendous service to you, and that it helps you enjoy one of the greatest gifts known to humanity.

Treasure the gift of being a mom!
Kristine Carlson

THE DON'T SWEAT GUIDE
FOR MOMS

1.

Defining Mother

The dictionary definition of mother is "a female parent." But in fact, the true definition of a mother encompasses so much more. A mother is also a teacher, a caregiver, and a nurse. She is a storyteller, a scientist, and an artist. She is a chauffeur, a chef, a soccer coach, and sometimes, even a father! A mother is compassionate, strong, independent, and courageous. She is loving, nurturing, and resilient.

Miraculously, mothers take on the job without any formal training. Their tour of duty begins from the moment that they become pregnant. They forge ahead without an official rulebook or set of instructions. A mother learns her skills only by trial and error—from her nine-month pregnancy well into her child's college years. And whether she is a working mother or a stay-at-home mom, she is nevertheless *always* on active duty! Whether she's preparing for labor, rocking a baby to sleep, shuttling her kids from school to dance lessons three times a week, or back-to-school shopping for freshman year, as clichéd as it sounds, there is no arguing with the facts: A mother's work is never done.

Yes, it's exhausting. And no, there isn't a big fat paycheck at the end of the work week. But the rewards of motherhood are plentiful, to say the least. A kiss from a grateful daughter, a smile from an appreciative son, or a heartfelt thank-you from a teenager can be great rewards. In what other capacity can a woman complete an exasperating work week and find such enormous satisfaction in little pleasures such as these?

2.

New Mom Anxiety

"New mom anxiety" occurs on a daily basis, thanks to the unpredictability of having a new baby at home. The overwhelming demands of a baby, unrealistic expectations, and an exhaustion so severe that you can barely remember what day it is, are enough to prevent you from ever making it out of the house!

Luckily, there are ways that a new mother can cope with the stress. Simple, practical techniques can reduce anxiety, increase your energy level, and help you derive more enjoyment out of time with your baby.

The easiest form of stress reduction is learning how to breathe! When we're anxious, we tend to take smaller breaths, which withholds oxygen from our cells and releases stress hormones. When you feel anxious, stop and take a slow, deep breath, counting to four as you breathe in. Pause, then exhale, counting back slowly as you let the breath out. Repeat this a few times, and then return to what you were doing.

Experts have found that women with a strong support system are at a lower risk of stress, not to mention heart disease. Sometimes, just being able to get together for a few hours a week to talk to other mothers will help you feel less tense. Learn that you aren't the only woman in the world who feels so overwhelmed and tired all the time.

Positive thinking is another method for reducing new mom anxiety. Negative thoughts seem to plague new moms. These thoughts can increase stress and anxiety, and can even bring about depression. It's important to restructure your negative thinking, analyzing each negative thought and working to change it into a positive one.

If you don't take care of yourself, you'll never be able to take care of your baby properly. For the first few months, you may have devoted every hour to taking care of your infant. If you've fallen into the trap of being a mother who denies her own needs, both you and your family will eventually suffer. Your baby *doesn't* need your attention every waking minute of the day. In fact, she can start learning that other people can care for her, too.

Begin by giving yourself permission to take some time for yourself. Many mothers feel tremendously guilty when they leave their baby in someone else's care. Set the guilt aside and take time to attend your needs. Get a haircut or a manicure, go to the driving range and hit a bucket of balls, schedule a massage—it doesn't matter *what* you do as long as you focus on caring for yourself. By treating yourself with compassion and care, you'll become better able to *give* compassion and care! You'll be a better mother for it.

3.

From Day One

The moment of birth is like nothing that you've ever experienced, but imagine how it feels for your new baby! It must come as a great shock to your newborn, who is having many new experiences: lights, sounds, smells, the touch of cold air. The most comforting thing that you can do is to hold the baby against your warm body. Your womb was all the baby knew and depended on for nine months. Now that the birth has taken place, the baby will depend on you for everything else!

Since some newborns can have certain unexpected characteristics, it's important to realize that these characteristics are usually temporary and no cause for concern. For instance, if your baby was born vaginally, the head may have a funny shape or be swollen as a result of having been squeezed through the birth canal. Or there may be dull pink patches on the neck, forehead, or eyelids, thanks to swollen blood vessels. These all disappear after a while.

Your newborn may be tired after the ordeal of being born; or ravenous and need to suck; or unusually quiet, observing all the new sights and sounds. Hold the baby and begin talking right away —your new child needs to learn the sound of your voice and the smell and feel of your body. Then pass the baby along to Daddy to learn his voice and smell, as well.

If you'll be breastfeeding, you can begin nursing in the delivery room if your baby is hungry. Your first milk—called colostrum—is thinner and more watery than breast milk, but it's rich in antibodies that will protect your newborn from infections. In a few days, the colostrum will be replaced by breast milk.

If you've given birth at a hospital, you'll be permitted to stay anywhere from twenty-four to forty-eight hours, until your doctor and your baby's pediatrician have determined that you're both in good shape to go home. Prepare yourself for periodic checkups during the first twenty-four hours after giving birth—you'll probably be poked and prodded twice as much as you were during labor! Discuss any questions or concerns that you may have with your doctor—you are sure to experience some bizarre bodily functions during this recuperating time, most of which are completely routine.

Most important, get as much rest as you can! Your body has just been put through a major workout and needs ample time to heal. The key to keeping your energy level high is to get plenty of sleep while your baby sleeps—some old but good advice. Then you'll be ready and alert to give your newborn love, comfort, and attention during the baby's first few days of life!

4.

Surviving That First Week

You'll be sent home from the hospital within two to three days after giving birth, but your body will take much longer to adjust to not being pregnant. While it does, take it as easy as you can and save your energy for meeting the demands of that new little miracle asleep in the bassinet.

Week number one brings many changes, both physical and emotional, and every change is completely natural. You may find that you go from happy to sad in the blink of an eye. Changing levels of hormones in your body, fatigue, and the isolation many new mothers feel at home during that first week can account for those mood swings.

One way to help yourself adapt to these changes is to accept as much support as you can find. If you're nursing, contact a lactation consultant to help you through the rough times. If your mother, sister, or mother-in-law offers to stay over and help out, accept immediately, even if that person's presence usually makes you anxious. You'll be overwhelmed with a new baby—feedings, changings, laundry. Even a normally meddling mother-in-law will be a welcome sight for your exhausted eyes.

Many new mothers—even those who have thoroughly prepared themselves for pregnancy, labor, and delivery—fail to prepare themselves for the first week. You're going to feel sore. You're going to hurt a lot. It's going to be tough making that first bowel movement, and tough just walking from room to room if you're recovering from an episiotomy. You're going to bleed, leak, and be uncomfortable. Your ankles may swell as a result of an epidural, and your breasts will throb when your milk comes in.

The best advice is to prepare yourself well ahead of time. Pay a visit to the drugstore before you deliver, and stock up on such items as sanitary napkins, nursing pads, ice packs, witch hazel, antibiotic cream, Preparation H, and suppositories. Make sure you have enough to avoid sending your husband out at all hours of the night!

Finally, just as you need your partner's help and support during this chaotic time, he needs the same from you. Men often have less experience with babies than women—but don't let this fact cause you to take over. Make sure Dad has ample opportunity and encouragement to care for his baby. In the first few weeks of your baby's life, nothing is certain except that everything changes. It is an unavoidable part of being a new parent!

5.

Mommy 101

For some new mothers, beginning life with a new baby comes easy. They seem to know exactly what to do and when to do it. It all comes naturally for them, as if they've been mothers for years.

But for most new moms, every little thing related to your baby presents a challenge. What diapers should I buy? How long should I nurse? Can I use a Q-tip in the baby's ear, or not? Learning to adjust to life with a baby can be rocky, to say the least, especially when you throw sleep deprivation, frequent feedings, lack of freedom, and bouts of crying into the mix. Though there's no official course on mothering, there is a source of information and help out there that every new mom should take advantage of: other mothers!

No one knows what being a mom really means until it happens. You're awakened from a deep sleep three or four times a night. There are days you don't shower before four o'clock. It's very stressful to be a new parent. You're often anxious about your new role and whether you're doing things right. That's why it's essential to turn to fellow moms—for sharing ideas, advice, or emotional support. With such support, a new mom should realize that what she's going through is not unusual, and more importantly, that she's not going through it alone.

A mother's group or playgroup benefits both mother and baby enormously. For moms, it's a place where they know that they'll find support. For babies, it's their first exposure to the outside world. Sure, at first, they'll all just look at each other and exchange a few smiles, but as they grow, there will be plenty of interaction. Your baby will learn skills from other babies, teach different skills to the other babies, and become a real social butterfly—and so will you!

6.

You and Your Baby

It's important for new mothers to know that in the beginning, there will be a lot of trial and error involved in caring for your baby. As long as the baby is always handled gently and with love, you shouldn't be afraid of making mistakes. So what if you put a diaper on backward? Who cares if the snaps on the onesie are a tad messed up? Go with your instincts, and if it feels right and seems to work—keep it up! After a day or so, you'll be a pro! Now read on for a quick guide to other baby basics.

Holding baby. Don't let anybody tell you that if you hold your baby too much, he will get spoiled. It's impossible to spoil a newborn. When holding the infant, always support the neck and head, regardless of the position in which the baby is being held. Try a few different positions at first, to find the one that you're most comfortable with. Swaddle your baby before holding him—it'll make him feel safer and warmer. Swaddling is wrapping your baby snugly in a blanket. A nurse at the hospital can help you learn to swaddle properly.

Burping baby. Babies typically get fussy if they've swallowed air during feeding. A good strategy is to burp her frequently during feedings, even if she shows no discomfort. There are quite a few techniques used to burp a newborn. The most effective positions include holding the baby upright with her head on your shoulder and gently patting her back with your other hand, or sitting her on your lap and supporting her chest and head with one hand, while gently patting her back with the other.

Diapering baby. With a little practice, you'll be able to change even the messiest diaper under the most undesirable conditions— such as on the side of the highway in the trunk of the car, or in the bathroom of a fancy restaurant. It's a good idea to be prepared and have everything at hand before removing the baby's diaper. Never leave a baby on a changing table unattended.

Dressing baby. Dressing a baby in *any* outfit can be quite a challenge! According to the Academy of Pediatrics, the most efficient way to dress a baby is to support him on your lap, and then stretch the garment neckline and pull it over his head. Use your fingers to keep it from catching on his face and ears. Instead of trying to push his arm through a sleeve, put your hand through the sleeve from the outside and pull his hand gently through.

Before long, holding, burping, dressing, and diapering will come so naturally that you'll laugh at having ever worried about them. Then you'll have more time to worry about the real tough stuff—like how to trim those unbelievably small fingernails!

7.

The Pregnant Mind and Body

Mood swings, insecurities, fears, forgetfulness—all of these and more will likely surface during your pregnancy, often at unpredictable times. Why do you sometimes feel so out of control while you're expecting?

One word: hormones! Hormonal surges can cause your emotions to fluctuate wildly. The fact that a baby is on the way is a momentous life change. You've become a walking receptacle of feelings, with no ability to suppress any of them. How can you gain enough control to make it?

Try being a little easier on yourself. Nobody's perfect, and no expectant mother has ever had a problem-free pregnancy. Every woman with a baby on board has experienced some form of emotional upheaval. If you learn to expect the roller coaster of emotions during pregnancy, you'll be better prepared to handle them when they pop up out of nowhere.

Stop worrying. It's difficult not knowing what the future holds, or being apprehensive about the pending labor, delivery, and *pain*

—but giving in to these anxieties will only create stress. Discussing your fears with your partner or doctor may help relieve some of your anxiety.

Talk to other mothers. Ask them how they cope or how they manage with a new baby at home. Financial burdens and health issues can be extremely taxing for expecting mothers, but sharing your concerns with other women in the same boat can ease the burden—especially when you realize that you're not alone.

8.

You and Your Spouse

Among the many changes women undergo when they become parents are those—some of them drastic—that they will face within their marriage. What was once a twosome is now a threesome, and that third party—no matter how sweet, wonderful, and cuddly—can be extremely demanding on the family unit. New babies have a talent for disrupting schedules, cutting into couple time, and depriving hardworking parents of much-needed sleep. Though it's common for marital relationships to suffer in the first few months after a baby is born, and though many parents even expect and wait for it to happen, when it does, it is still tremendously difficult to face.

Complicating matters are the feelings each parent may have that he or she is working harder or sacrificing more than the other for the needs of the family. This almost always breeds feelings of resentment and contempt.

For many new mothers, these feelings are extreme, especially if they are the chosen parent who stays home with baby while their husbands go off to work. Feelings of "doing all of the work without any paycheck" or being left out of adult life often surface. Spouses who do go to work often feel left out of the child-rearing process and burdened by the family's financial obligations.

The bottom line is that taking care of a new baby is both thrilling and demanding. Both parents are challenged to perform unfamiliar tasks. The only way to get through most of them is to learn to work together as a team and negotiate the new issues.

Rather than resort to harsh words, couples who talk out these issues and are sensitive to each other's needs can learn to share responsibilities and alleviate some of the pressure both parties are experiencing. More importantly, couples need time alone after they've begun a family, to reconnect with each other every so often. Couples need to share their feelings and focus on practical issues such as schedules, how responsibilities can be shared, and when to solicit outside help. Holding it all in just builds resentment toward each other.

9.

Getting Back into Shape

No matter how much weight you put on during your pregnancy, once the baby is out, you're going to weigh less! Unfortunately, most of the weight lost after delivery is baby and placenta weight. For many women, the challenge is just beginning: having to lose upwards of twenty pounds or more. Many new moms worry excessively over losing this weight.

Losing your "baby weight" can be done—but keep in mind that very few women get their body shapes back to the way they were before pregnancy. The important thing is losing weight and feeling fit. Maintaining a healthy attitude about your body and food will set you on the right track to proper fitness after pregnancy.

Rule #1: Eat in response to hunger. Many of us eat out of boredom or frustration. Instead, try using food for what it's intended for— nutrition, sustenance, and energy. If you're bored, leave the house, even if it's just for a walk around the block. If you're frustrated, reach for the telephone instead of the fridge, and call a friend for support.

Rule #2: Control your portions. We're taught at a young age to eat everything on our plates. That's fine if you can regulate your portions. Also, steer clear of watching TV or reading while you eat. It's harder to keep track of how much you're eating while you're focusing on something else.

Rule #3: Wait six weeks. Check with your doctor in regard to how long you should wait before exercising after delivery. You want to make sure that your uterus has had ample time to return to its normal size. There are no rules about when and how much to exercise—that depends largely on how fit you were before and during pregnancy, and the nature of your delivery. In combination with an aerobic workout (running, walking, swimming, biking, and so on), strength training will help speed up your post-pregnancy weight loss. Yoga can stretch your muscles and ease your mind, as well as improve your posture, which may have changed since pregnancy.

As a new mom, it's essential to know the importance of praising yourself and keeping a positive self-image. Regardless of your weight, if you're a good person and a loving mother, you are beautiful, no matter the size of your body.

10.

Pink and Blue Blues

Most new mothers experience changes in their moods soon after childbirth. The "postpartum blues" or "baby blues," develop two to four days after delivery and can be accompanied by insomnia, exhaustion, and confusion. Fortunately, postpartum blues are usually mild and short-lived—clearing up after just a few days —and they are considered part of the normal birth recovery process. Taking good care of yourself, both physically and mentally, is sometimes all that's needed to end the baby blues.

Postpartum is similar to the blues, but more intense. Some women may feel unable to cope with the demands of a newborn. Others withdraw from their family and friends, stop eating or start overeating, or simply become unable to function.

With postpartum depression, it's normal for a woman to feel a roller coaster of emotions with a new baby. The key is to be able to ask for medical help if those few days of the blues turn into weeks or months. If you or someone you know shows signs of severe postpartum depression, make sure to tell your doctor.

11

Are You Mother of the Year?

With proper time management, you may not be able to altogether avoid the chaos that a new baby brings, but you can surely learn how to maximize the time you have and make the most of those precious minutes.

The first order of business in time management is to assess your time. Look closely at how you spend your time. It may surprise you to know that most people spend up to an hour a day on tasks that could be put on hold or eliminated completely.

The second step is to prioritize. Put that "to do" list you've been keeping in your head down on paper, and then divide your chores into three parts: things that need to be taken care of immediately, things that can get done anytime during the week, and long-term projects.

Keep one step ahead of the game: Try setting the table for dinner in the afternoon after unloading the dishwasher. Prepare baby bottles the night before. Select your children's clothes for the following day the night before.

Learn to multitask: Consolidate jobs and get things done during downtime. One of the best purchases you can make when you have an infant is a telephone headset. With a headset, your hands will be free to do other things.

Always, always ask for help. When you're running short on time, ask a friend to baby-sit your child in exchange for baby-sitting hers sometime. It's amazing how much you'll be able to get done in a couple of hours.

Organize your home. One of the biggest time-wasters is looking for lost items. Even if you're in a hurry to add the fabric softener, make sure to put those house keys back on their hook before running down to the basement.

And finally, the ultimate time management tip: Stop trying to do it all! Decide what you can live with and what you can't live without. Maybe the laundry can wait until tomorrow—if it means you'll have some extra time to blow-dry your hair today!

12.

Indulge in a Massage

There's a little-known pleasure that many pregnant women indulge in that can drastically make a difference in the way you feel physically during your pregnancy. It's called a maternity massage, and if you've never had one, then run to the nearest therapy center!

Can you imagine actually feeling *physically* good despite the fact that your body is larger than a small village and your energy level is at an all-time low? It can happen—and all it takes is a phone call to a licensed massage therapist.

Some people assume that a massage is just another expensive way to be pampered. Not so! Soft-tissue massage is a legitimate form of physical therapy for pregnant women. It can help to relax tense muscles and alleviate undue strain and injury to ligaments and joints. If you're carrying some thirty pounds of extra weight, your back is likely strained beyond belief—not to mention all of the excess stress on your legs and feet.

It might surprise you to learn that many insurance policies include chiropractic care and cover massage therapy within that care. Some policies cover massage therapy well into postpartum, so check with your carrier.

You'll also be surprised to learn that most massage tables can be adjusted to accommodate that big belly of yours. Some massage tables are even designed with the pregnant woman in mind, with stretch material in the midsection. This allows you to lie on your stomach so that the therapist can really work on that aching back. Once you've exhausted all comfortable positions with the eleven pillows you've been sleeping with lately, you may find that this table is the answer to your prayers!

13.

Milk Spoils, Babies Don't

When your baby cries, you may automatically pick him up and console him. But chances are that if older relatives or friends are around when this happens, *somebody* is going to say, "Don't pick him up every time he cries! You'll spoil him!"

However, the notion of spoiling an infant is outdated. Babies can't be spoiled. They can't verbalize their needs any other way than by crying. How insensitive would it be for a new mother to ignore her baby's request for nourishment or a clean diaper?

Crying in the first six months is not a manipulative act by a baby. The more quickly you meet your baby's needs to be fed or changed or held, the more secure and content he's going to feel. Wouldn't you like a secure, happy, and well-fed baby?

When your baby passes the six-month mark, *then* it may be time to set a few limits. But for the first few months of life, your baby needs all the nurturing he can get from you in order to build strong self-esteem.

14.

Will I Ever Sleep Again?

Once you have children, sleep as you know it has changed forever, especially during the first few months. Babies need to eat, and they need to eat a lot—even at three in the morning. But by the time your baby turns five months old, she should be able to go through the night without having to nurse or drink a bottle.

That doesn't necessarily mean that she's going to sleep through the night, though. One of the hardest tasks that new parents face in the first year of a baby's life is getting her to sleep through the night —or, at least for four hours in a row. And just because your daughter slept through the night five nights in a row, you may now think that she has a routine. But the next night she may be up again—this time, three times during the night.

Babies do not understand that the world is a bigger place than what they see. So when Mommy and Daddy put them in the crib and leave the room, they don't realize that they're coming back. Babies feel hurt and abandoned, and some go on to cry for hours.

It could take weeks, or even months, to teach your baby to fall asleep comfortably and sleep through every night. Even then, there are no guarantees. But there are some guidelines you can use to help set the wheels in motion for a good night's sleep for everyone.

Routines are best—even for very little babies during the first few weeks of life. Every night before bed, give your baby a bath, dress her in pajamas, read a book or talk to her softly, and then nurse her until she gets sleepy. When her eyes are glazed over and her eyelids are heavy, put her in her crib. Do the exact same thing the same way every night.

Put her to sleep in the same place every time. This may be difficult for babies in daycare, but it's been proven effective to put a baby down—even for naps—in the same place. This way, she learns that when she is put down in the crib, it is time to go to sleep.

Make sure to conduct all pre-bedtime activity in your baby's room. As she gets older, she will learn by association. If you get her ready for bed in her room every night, she will understand that it's bedtime. In fact, your baby's room should really be used only for sleeping. The last thing you want is for your baby to associate her room with playtime.

15.

The Diaper Bag

To be a true super mom, you'll first need to buy a super diaper bag. Keep in mind that this bag is going to be used and abused, sometimes stuffed beyond capacity, and toted through all kinds of weather. Select a dark-colored, nylon diaper bag—many handbag designers now design diaper bags that look great and are very functional.

You'll definitely need a bag that comes with a changing pad to avoid having to lay your baby down on hard surfaces. Also, always keep a cloth diaper folded within the changing pad to protect the pad itself from messy changes. Pack along a couple of extra cloth diapers for burping, spitting up, and other messes. Never use the cloth diaper from the pad for any other purpose—you don't want germs from diaper changes anywhere near your baby's face.

A plastic travel pack filled with wipes enables easy access to baby wipes and can be refilled every day. Take along a thick stack of wipes every time that you leave the house—they aren't just for the baby, but for cleaning your hands, as well. Diaper-rash cream, baby sunblock, and powder (corn starch) are good items to have, too. Don't forget to leave room for at least one of your baby's favorite toys, a favorite comfort object, and a bib.

Take two bottles, if your baby uses them—one made, and one ready to make. You may want to put the nipples in a separate plastic bag to keep things sanitary. Two extra pacifiers can also be kept in that plastic bag.

If your baby is on solids, take along take a container of baby food and a spoon. If he's a little older, keep plenty of snacks (Cheerios, crackers, and the like) on hand. You should also squeeze in a large bottle of water for every outing—not only for drinking, but for washing off that pacifier or bottle that will inevitably fall on the ground.

Some extras you may want to think about, should you still have room: your cell phone for emergencies, an index card with important phone numbers (spouse, pediatrician, neighbor), and plenty of plastic bags for sealing and tossing dirty diapers or taking home soiled clothes. Of course, don't forget the diapers!

16.

What'll We Call the Baby?

When there's a baby on the way, the mother and father must agree on a name for the infant. Everybody has their own ideas about names that they like. Now with additional factors involved—a spouse's strong opinion, religious reasons, tradition—the baby naming becomes a family debate rooted in compromise.

New parents best keep one thing in mind when plowing through the baby name books: Your little one is going to have to live with the name that you choose forever, so you may want to stay clear of too many hyphens, untraditional spellings, and names that are too difficult to pronounce. Above all, don't let outside pressure from parents or in-laws affect your decision!

What you *should* do is have fun with naming the baby! Search the Internet for baby-naming sites, skim classic novels for name ideas, or even check out the soaps! In the event that you still can't decide upon a decent name, there's always Michael or Jessica, which have been among the most popular names for the past decade.

17.

Mommy & Me

There's much to be said about participating in a Mommy & Me program with your baby. Your baby, even at three months, can gain a lot from the experience, plus it can be very rewarding for you. Most Mommy & Me classes offer an atmosphere conducive to your baby's age and developmental stage, and provide structured, interactive activities for you and your baby to share.

You can find a Mommy & Me class by checking your local YMCA, church, or synagogue. These classes are usually led by certified early child care professionals and are offered for all ages. Most instructors provide age-appropriate equipment such as mats, balls, bubbles, and dolls—all of which will delight and stimulate your little one.

Don't expect your three-month-old to interact with the other three-month-olds in her class, but at this young age you'll be surprised at how much she wants to interact with *you*! She'll come to recognize certain songs and finger plays and react with a smile, and she may eventually show recognition of her surroundings when you arrive for class each time.

It's a good idea for moms to participate in a trial Mommy & Me class before signing up, just to make sure that the environment is right. Check out the other moms in the class, where they're from, and how they interact with their babies. Many Mommy & Me classes are divided into two parts: The first half of the class is often comprised of interactive exercises for mother and child, and the second half is an organized discussion between the mothers, led by the instructor. These discussions offer new moms the opportunity to share stories, experiences, and advice with other moms, and often help to form a wonderful Mommy support network and long-lasting friendships!

The class you ultimately choose should offer plenty of music, interactive games, and colorful floor equipment to stimulate your baby both physically and mentally. Most importantly, check for cleanliness. Ask the instructor how often the equipment is cleaned, and make sure that it meets all safety requirements. Both you and your baby should dress appropriately for class—in comfortable, moveable clothing with no zippers or sharp objects.

Lastly, remember to bring a camera or camcorder to one of your classes. You can ask the instructor or one of the other mothers to record you and your baby participating in the different activities. Won't Daddy be thrilled to see how much fun his little girl is having at school!

18.

If I Have to Eat One More Saltine...

"**M**orning sickness" is a complete misnomer! For some, morning sickness lasts all day! The best thing that can be said about "first trimester nausea" is that while the nausea lasts throughout pregnancy for some women, the majority of pregnant woman only experience it anywhere from their eighth week through their fourteenth week.

First trimester nausea is caused by the sudden changes in a woman's hormone levels. It's more common in the first trimester because that's when your body is typically going through these changes. By the time they have leveled out (usually by the start of the second trimester), your body has become used to the changes.

Unfortunately, some women find that nothing helps relieve their discomfort. For others, different techniques may offer relief at different times.

Frequent snacking and drinking a lot of water has provided many women with the antidote to nausea. Small doses of bland foods, such as whole-grain crackers and broth, will help to combat nausea. If you can't bear to look at another cracker, try replacement snacks that offer the same comfort, such as whole-wheat bread, pretzels, or bagels. Avoid spicy foods and stringy foods like spaghetti, and chew your food thoroughly.

Make sure to take your vitamins. The general consensus by most obstetricians is that prenatal vitamins are important to your health and your baby's health. Some women experience even more nausea when taking vitamins. If you fall in that category, speak to your doctor about getting a prenatal vitamin that won't make you sick. Sometimes, an additional supplement of B6 and magnesium can offer help for nauseous mothers-to-be.

Most importantly, be prepared! Carry plastic bags and breath mints with you at all times (just in case)! Keep a supply of peanut butter crackers or trail mix on hand to munch on periodically. In addition, keep snacks on your nightstand for late-night nausea and for munching on when you wake up.

Lastly, it's important that you keep yourself hydrated. Everyone is different, so experiment with what works best for you. Remember, the day will come when you won't feel as though you're on a dinghy sailing through rough waters!

19.

Grownups: Please Call!

Sometimes, the strain of being the only adult at home for days on end can be tremendous. You long for some mature, adult interaction—so much so that you'll even sign up for new phone service just to have a longer conversation with the long-distance solicitor. It's worse if you live in colder regions. Frequent snowstorms mean cabin fever, and days of cabin fever can result in bundling up the baby and trekking through five-foot-high snowdrifts just to interact with other adult human beings.

Playgroups don't address this specific need—sure, they get you out of the house and give you ample opportunity to talk to other women, but most of the time, you're interrupted by the needs of the children just when you get a conversation going. Worse still, playgroup conversations almost always revolve around the kids.

When you finally know that it's time to spend a little more time with adults only, and a little less time with your beloved children, arrange a girls' night out with some friends and go for coffee or drinks and grown-up conversation. Or start a monthly book club, and have a discussion with other mothers about literature that doesn't involve a hungry caterpillar, a runaway bunny, or a curious monkey.

The important thing to remember is that all stay-at-home moms need a little break from their children every once in a while: time to relax and think straight; time to talk about anything besides nursing and diapers; time to rediscover current events and fine art; just time for themselves.

20.

Mother Knows Breast

The American Academy of Pediatrics recommends that mothers breastfeed their babies for the first year, but that isn't always feasible, or even desirable. Sometimes, baby begins weaning himself long before then, and sometimes, mom just "wants her body back" and decides that it's time to stop.

If you think that you're ready to begin weaning your baby, chances are that you are. To make the process as comfortable as possible for you and your baby, ask your doctor for some advice on how to begin. Discuss the procedure with other mothers who have weaned, and decide on the strategy that is right for you.

It helps to gradually introduce your baby to supplemental bottles, replacing one breastfeeding session with one bottle every day. If you've already started supplementing breast milk with an occasional bottle, weaning may have already begun. If your baby is older than nine months, doctors recommend weaning straight to a sippy cup, rather than to a bottle. Babies this age usually have the dexterity and skill to manage a cup with a secure lip.

If you've begun supplementing with a bottle and your baby is having a problem, you may want to try changing nipples. Newly developed orthodontic nipples are designed to be kinder to a baby's developing mouth and easier to suck. Try different nipple holes, too —some babies have an easier time sucking from a slanted hole rather than from a traditional, round hole.

Now the hard part: Prepare yourself for the pain of engorgement! Unfortunately, this is a side effect of weaning that mothers must endure. Your breasts will feel hard and uncomfortably full. It's possible, too, that you may run a low-grade fever. Don't return to nursing, however. This will confuse your baby and delay the weaning process. Instead, use cold compresses and take acetaminophen to relieve the pain.

Weaning your baby can be one of the most stressful, emotional times for you—and psychologically, it can be traumatic. But you love your baby with every ounce of your being. You're not going to stop bonding just because you stop nursing. There are many ways for you and your baby to bond, and you can still share intimate moments together doing other things.

Try to keep all stress to a minimum when weaning, so as not to place any undue stress on your baby. And be patient—some babies initially refuse to drink from a bottle for a number of reasons—but in time, he will drink and continue to flourish. Rest assured—he will always want to be held!

21.

Clothing Fit for a Circus

No matter what body type you have, maternity clothes *can* look nice on you. When putting together your maternity wardrobe, try these simple fashion tricks to help you look great throughout your pregnancy.

Get yourself four or five A-line, cotton shirts, two long-sleeved and two short-sleeved. Depending on which season you will be at your largest, select one more—long-sleeved for fall and winter, short-sleeved for spring and summer. These don't necessarily have to be maternity shirts—you can find comfortable A-line tops in any women's department store. An A-line shirt is extra-roomy at the lower half and complements any pregnant figure. It also fits forever! A well-made, comfortable A-line blouse can be worn in your first or ninth month. Try black and white, which will match everything.

Splurge for those maternity leggings. They may cost a bit more, but you'll live in them. The elastic waistband and roomy tummy area are perfect for everyday wear, well into the last trimester. They'll also make comfortable pajama bottoms in the weeks following your delivery! They'll look great paired with your A-line tops.

Raiding your husband's closet is a good bet. Men's shirts over leggings or extra-large T-shirts over maternity shorts will save you from spending a lot of money on clothes.

Chances are that by your eighth month of pregnancy, you'll be sick to death of your wardrobe, and nothing that you bought early on will even fit. It may not make sense to buy more maternity clothes with only a few weeks to go, but this is actually the perfect time to treat yourself to three more outfits! It'll be a strain on your wallet, but it's worth it if the new clothes make you feel good during the home stretch of your pregnancy. Just remember to choose casual clothes that can be worn *after* you give birth, too.

Most importantly, remember that comfort is the key to maternity dressing. These days, maternity wear can be hip and fashionable. Stick to the look that you feel most comfortable with, and maybe you'll have fewer of those teary-eyed mornings, staring hopelessly into your closet, wondering what's going to fit!

22.

Make the Most of Maternity Leave

There's no way to completely make the transition of going back to work a smooth one. You're bound to encounter bumps along the way—separation anxiety, adjusting to a new nanny or daycare, re-entering the working world, and the inevitable daily stress that comes with trying to leave work early enough to pick up your baby. The best thing that you can do to alleviate some of the anxiety is to begin preparing for your return to work a week or two after coming home from the hospital. Yes, that early!

If you've chosen to have a nanny care for your baby (and you should begin the interview process well ahead of time), get her started two weeks prior to your work return date. This will give you ample time to get to know one another, and an opportunity for you to see if you are comfortable with her method of care. You'll have time to iron out any problems and teach her the way that you like things done. You'll also be able to practice leaving your baby for short periods of time each day, building up to the day where you can leave her for a full workday.

Should you opt for a daycare center for your baby, it's a good idea to enroll her in the program a good two weeks before you have to be back at work. Just as if you had hired a nanny, by giving you and the baby two weeks to adjust, you can make the transition easier by leaving her a little longer each day and working up to a full day. You'll also have a decent amount of time to decide if you like the center that you've chosen.

Returning to work will be extremely difficult at first, but try shifting your focus away from the sadness you feel and toward the time you'll have at home to spend with your baby. Make the most of that time together by going for late afternoon walks or trips to the playground before dinner. Keep yourself in the most relaxed mode possible, and treasure every single minute. Then think about this: The two hours of undivided attention that you are devoting to your child each day are probably more quality time than many mothers find to spend with their kids!

23.

The Mother's Load

Even in the most modern families, when it comes to child-care chores, Mom usually ends up doing more of the work. That remains true, in most cases, whether Mom is a stay-at-home mom or a working mom. Dad bows to Mom in the first few weeks of a baby's life, with the notion that she knows exactly what she's doing and he'll just get in the way.

When confronted with the facts, most men will admit to doing less. But it's not for a lack of trying. Many men honestly don't know what they're doing, haven't been taught the proper ways to do things, and hate the feelings of inadequacy that result from having Mom always take over. Women need to learn how to be patient teachers if they want their husbands to contribute more.

It's a good idea to establish steadfast rules when it comes to sharing parenting responsibilities. If your infant is waking in the middle of the night, Mom can't be expected to get up with him every night, then again every morning, bright and early. Start sharing this duty by selecting a mutually agreed upon time—say, five in the morning. Then should the baby cry before five, for instance, Dad has to coax him back to sleep. Anytime after five, and it's Mom's responsibility.

Establish a set routine, and then split the week or the weekend into two parts: Mom can be responsible for the first half, and Dad for the second. This way, you both know what to expect and when to expect it, and you can relax more during your off-days.

Setting a certain time to do something with your child not only benefits you by providing regrouping time, but it helps your child feel a sense of familiarity. When Dad comes home from work, have him establish a ritual of giving your toddler a bath. He'll get to decompress and share some special bonding time with his child, and you know you have every evening at that time to do something other than take care of the baby.

It's important, too, when learning to share responsibilities, to accept Daddy's limitations—his braids are not going to look like your braids, and his scrambled eggs will probably taste different than yours. You're both going to have different approaches toward everything, and you need to respect that. If he's pulling his weight with the child-care chores—even if you have plenty to say about how he's getting them done—just keep quiet and learn to be appreciative. Relax and let Dad do his job!

24.

Preparing for the Big Event

The last thing an expectant mother wants is to arrive at the hospital, only to realize she's forgotten something—the baby's first outfit, a toothbrush, or that paperback that she'll probably never get to open anyway. Since looming labor and delivery breeds major forgetfulness, it's best to be prepared well in advance for when that first contraction comes. If there are things that you must absolutely have with you at the hospital, make sure to include them on a list. It can be frustrating to the breaking point to be ready to push and realize that you've forgotten the one hair clip that keeps your hair off of your face.

When packing your hospital bag for the big event, choose a bag that's lightweight and try not to stuff it to capacity. The essentials are a comfortable robe, two old nightgowns or pajama tops that you don't mind getting messy, warm socks, slippers, a comfortable outfit that you can wear home (perhaps one of your early maternity outfits), sanitary pads, toiletries, and hair accessories.

Make a little room for a few things Dad may need at the hospital. Pack a change of clothes, a book or magazine, a toothbrush and other toiletries, some cash and change for snacks and phone calls, and a watch for timing contractions.

If there's still room, you'll need some of the baby's essentials. Should your bag be full, it's a good idea to make a separate bag for baby. Yes, it's more luggage to think about, but get used to it! The baby is going to be taking up most of your luggage and trunk space from now on!

For the baby, pack a few receiving blankets, two "onesies," two pairs of socks, a newborn hat, and a "going home" outfit (which should include a sweater or bunting if the weather is cold).

Make sure to pack your important documents, as well. You may need insurance cards, your address book, and your social security cards, among other things.

Lastly, the most important thing to have is an infant car seat. No hospital will allow you to leave without one. Just make sure that you and your partner have practiced putting the seat into the car and removing it before the big day!

25.

Top Ten Things to Do at 3 A.M.

It seems that new mothers find themselves awake for some reason or other at all hours of the night. Whether it's for that late-night feeding or those trips to the nursery to comfort a child with bad dreams, chances are that you've watched the clock go from three to four in the morning while you're wide awake—despite the fact that you're exhausted. Here are some ways to make that time productive—and combat your insomnia in the process!

1. Catch up on your e-mail. E-mail is the perfect invention for new parents—the best way to remain in touch with the outside world on your own time, even if that time is at 3:26 A.M.

2. Watch a video. If you're a parent, it's a good bet that your children have kept you from watching your favorite prime-time television show at one time or another. Tape your favorites, and watch them later on.

3. Get a jump on breakfast! Prepare your baby's bottles or sippy cups, or make a stack of pancakes that can be reheated in the morning. But try not to eat! Midnight snacking can be a hard habit to break.

4. Put a load in. It's amazing how much laundry a little baby makes. Get a load ahead!

5. How many nights have you stared longingly at that bestseller on your nightstand? Catch up on your reading, but remember to set a timer or you may find yourself reading straight through until morning.

6. Restock the changing table. Fill up the wipes carton, add diapers to your at-hand supply, and disinfect the changing pad.

7. Take time to plan out your monthly calendar in a neat and orderly fashion, including all your baby's play dates or classes. Make note of all of your appointments (doctor or hair) and baby-sitter visits.

8. Catch up on your correspondence. If you have a very new baby, you probably have a stack of thank-you cards waiting to be filled out, not to mention a pile of bills to be paid!

9. Fill those albums! Baby pictures fresh from the developer can sometimes accumulate to unearthly proportions! Start organizing (and dating) your pictures now.

10. Change over for the season. Are your child's drawers filled with clothes from last summer that don't fit anymore? Use your midnight hour to box up the clothes that don't fit, and pack away clothes for next year.

There you go—ten suggestions for ten nights of insomnia. Hopefully, after ten nights, your child will have passed through her "up at all hours" phase, and you can get some sleep!

26.

Babyproof Your Home

Even before your little one begins to crawl, the proper steps should be taken to ensure that your home is completely babyproof. In order to enjoy watching your child grow and learn as he explores, it is imperative that you make sure the environment is one hundred percent safe.

By far, the best way to babyproof your home is to call in a child safety expert who is professionally trained. He or she will be able to give you recommendations on what child safety products are necessary to eliminate the dangers. Some safety experts even offer to do the babyproofing for you at an additional cost.

There are two important things to remember when childproofing your home. The Child Safety Commission does not approve all of the child safety products on the market. It's essential to check to see which products have been approved before you purchase them.

The second thing to remember is that childproofing is an ongoing process. Certain measures that were not necessary when the baby was crawling are necessary as he learns to walk. You may need to call an expert in periodically to update your safety measures.

Babyproofing your home includes being aware of the following: Anything that is taller than it is wide can be pulled over on a child and cause injury. You should never leave a baby unattended in the bathtub, even for a minute. That's all it takes for a child to drown in one inch of water or less. Turn your hot water heater down to 120 degrees or lower to avoid burns.

Store all poisons and hazardous materials out of reach and locked away. Cleaning supplies, makeup, bath products, and vitamins need to be stored out of reach. (The number-one poisoning product is iron supplements.) Never place furniture under a window—children can use it to climb up on and fall out. Don't assume that a window screen will prevent your child from falling. You should also shorten all blind cords by wrapping them or cutting them to avoid possible strangulation.

The bottom line is that as parents, you need to commit yourselves to being aware of every safety issue that faces your baby. Ultimately, these concerns will help keep your child safe.

27.

Alternative Births

Once you get to the hospital, depending on how your labor progresses, there's always the chance that things may not go your way. You may be too far into labor for an epidural, or there may be complications that require a cesarean section. So even if you slapped down your twenty-five bucks for a six-week Lamaze course, you may never even get to take a breath.

Aside from a c-section, when you don't have a choice of birthing method, there are other methods that you and your partner can consider. The important thing to remember is that you, as the mom, must be completely comfortable with your chosen method. Never let anyone sway you one way or the other, based on their beliefs. That can lead to tremendous, undue stress on you and your unborn baby.

Whichever birthing method you choose, keep in mind that no one is going to judge you. Your biggest priorities should be your safety and comfort and the baby's health.

28.

It All Begins Here

You've been waiting and dreaming about this for months. You're pregnant. Your first order of business is making drastic changes to your lifestyle. You'll have to do this all over again when the baby comes in nine months, but for now, there are changes to make that you may not have even considered!

First, there are the obvious changes. Alcohol, cigarettes, and drugs of any kind are off-limits. But when your baby's health is at stake, it's best to make yourself aware of everything that might pose a threat. Coffee, cola, and chocolate (say it isn't so!) are all potentially problematic for your baby's health.

The key here is moderation. Studies are divided over how much caffeine may cause harm to your fetus. But why risk it? Limiting your amount of caffeine intake during pregnancy is your best bet. Try a half-cup of coffee in the morning, or blend your coffee with decaffeinated coffee. Switch to caffeine-free colas, and *try* to stay away from those truffles!

For many women, their pet cats are their children, too. However, cat feces can harbor a parasite that causes toxoplasmosis, the results of which can be devastating. But being pregnant doesn't mean you need to ship kitty off to a neighbor. It simply means that someone else needs to be in charge of the litter box for the next nine months. It's a good idea to wash your hands after cuddling or petting your cat, too. Experts also suggest staying away from children's sandboxes while you're pregnant—wandering cats sometimes use them as litter boxes.

Those are just a few of the dangers lurking to threaten your unborn baby's health. Expectant mothers need to beware of herbal remedies, hazardous household cleaners, saunas and hot tubs, secondhand smoke, vitamin A, and stress.

Being pregnant is one of the most exciting times of your life—but it can also be the most stressful. Remember to take care of yourself, and, of course, your baby. The rule is: If you have questions about anything, ask your obstetrician first!

29.

The Big Event

If you're expecting labor to be like it is on television or in the movies, where beautiful women "ooh" and "aah" a few times then scrunch up their faces and push out a baby without so much as a hair out of place, you're in for a bit of a surprise. In reality, labor can be a lot more painful—but you'll never know until you're actually going through it.

It helps to know the facts about labor, regardless of how yours is going to progress. And preparing yourself for a lot of pain and discomfort is a good idea—just think of how nice it will be to be prepared for a worst-case scenario and then experience less discomfort than you expected!

The truth is that most pregnant women study and prepare for this event as if it were the SATs. They pore over every book written about childbirth. They talk at length with their obstetrician. And they interview any and every family member who's been through it before. They've heard all the stories (horror and otherwise), and armed with ice chips and soothing music, a tennis ball for back pain and heavy socks for the anticipation of freezing feet, they make their way into the delivery room.

Still, how can you keep it together, knowing all too well what's about to happen? The best advice is to keep your stress level at a minimum. Remember that no two labors are alike, and just because your sister had back pain doesn't mean you're going to experience it, too. Try to remember this important bit of information—even as the pain and discomfort intensify, it's almost over! Your baby *will* come out! (They all do, eventually!)

Best of all, think about this: After all of the throbbing, the cramping, and the unbearable pressure, you're going to finally experience a *good* feeling—relief! When it's all said and done, you can forget all about contractions, dilating cervixes, and ice chips and relish what's really important: the amazing, new being you've just brought into this world!

30.

Running Errands with a Toddler

Since a toddler's social skills are constantly changing, a parent's coping skills need to keep up. Fortunately, many of the most trying developmental issues for the one-to-three set emerge at fairly predictable ages. With the right tools and the ability to second-guess your child, whether you're off to the supermarket, a restaurant, or a friend's house, you'll be prepared for anything.

In advance of any outing, consider your toddler's temperament and ask yourself the following questions:

How does he react to noise and crowds? Some children have no problem with loud music, bright lights, and a lot of people. Others can't handle them. A movie or a dentist's office may be torture for your toddler—try to avoid bringing your toddler to places such as these.

Has he napped? True, there are days that you really need to leave the house before your son's morning nap, but think twice about whether it's absolutely necessary. By scheduling activities after naptime, you'll both be happier and can avoid meltdowns.

Is he hungry? Even if you're headed for a restaurant with your toddler, it's a good idea to feed him before you leave the house. It's also a good idea to bring along some juice and light snacks to sustain him until the food actually comes to the table.

Is he familiar with where you are going? If you're on your way to a friend's house that you've never been to before, prepare your toddler for what he can expect there. Do they have a dog or a cat? Children? Do they live in an apartment building with an elevator? Anticipate all of the unfamiliar things he will encounter and prepare him as best you can.

What are his limits? Give yourself a smaller window of opportunity for shopping if you're bringing your little one—he doesn't have the stamina to hang around a shopping mall and will most likely grow bored if you're there for too long.

How prepared is your diaper bag? Never leave home for *any* outing without a few toys tucked into your diaper bag. Don't presume that a friend with older children will have toys for your son to play with. Don't assume that there are going to be exciting activities happening at the bank, either.

Finally, how are *you* feeling? If you have a throbbing headache, taking your toddler out on an errand is a *bad* idea. It's leaving the door wide open for impatience and frustration on both your parts. Postpone the errand, or if that's not possible, take some aspirin and delay it for a few hours.

31.

Beyond Cheerios

There are many mothers who dedicate most of their day trying to get their children to eat. Their children want one thing and one thing only—Cheerios. (Or perhaps in your house, it's hash browns, or strawberries.) For lunch, it's the same thing. By dinnertime, most exasperated mothers draw the line. Then what happens? The child eats nothing.

Fortunately, young children eventually grow out of this stage. By the time they are in kindergarten, they usually become real eaters. If your child seems to be eating nothing now, be patient. If she's happy, healthy, and somehow flourishing, don't worry. On the other hand, if she seems tired or cranky a lot or has a low energy level, check with your pediatrician about what you can do.

You may want to consider a few tricks of the trade to get your child to eat. Make dinnertime story time—read to her while she eats. Disguise vegetables—substitute butternut squash for potatoes and mash them. Or add pureed fruit to ice cream and yogurt.

Other tricks include serving dinner in a different place from time to time. A picnic outdoors can be fun. Make foods fun and colorful. Play silly games while you eat, incorporating eating into the game rules. Or change the traditional temperatures of foods to entice kids into thinking they're eating something off-the-wall: cold pizza, baked apples, frozen pasta — whatever works!

In the meantime, consider this: You could do a lot worse than Cheerios! Cheerios are actually pretty healthy, and contain a lot of nutritious ingredients. Paired with an apple and peanut butter — even a little bit — you've got a fairly healthy meal.

32.

A Single Mom Story

When it comes to single motherhood, there's no question that privileged, professional women have an advantage. Yet with proper planning, having a baby solo can be a viable option for those without that CEO job or hefty paycheck. In such cases, a good support system can be more valuable than a big bank account. Should any woman contemplate this path, there are many factors that should be considered.

Age is important. Experts recommend being at least thirty before considering single motherhood. Single mothers polled think that a woman shouldn't embark on single motherhood before thirty-five. The major consensus is that a woman shouldn't wait until forty, because of potential fertility problems.

Support from extended family members is also important. A single woman with supportive parents and siblings can help create a more nurturing family unit. Think about it this way: If you surround your child with family and love, he will be just as well off as other kids—and better off than kids from unhappy marriages.

You don't have to have millions in the bank to have a baby alone, but it helps to meet with a financial planner before making that decision. You'll also want to make sure that you create a proper will and trust, have a solid insurance policy in place, and appoint proper guardians.

Child care is obviously a huge concern for single mothers, especially since there is only that one paycheck coming in. Get creative—consider sharing nannies or offering to baby-sit for a friend's child on the weekend in exchange for the friend taking your child for one of the weekdays. Should you decide to become a single mother, also make sure to utilize the fantastic support groups out there.

Above all, make peace with yourself. Should you choose this less-than-traditional route and feel wracked with guilt and anxiety, you need to get over it! Get therapy if possible—anything to ensure that you are truly comfortable with your decision.

33.

The Perfect Carpool

With soccer, gymnastics, ballet, basketball, religious school, tap, piano lessons, hockey, chorus, baseball, tennis, and art as just *some* of the activities your children participate in, chances are that you are going find yourself the carpool driver every now and then. The average carpool ride doesn't last long, but there's still plenty of time for an emergency to strike. Are you prepared?

Even the most experienced drivers aren't immune to car accidents. The more prepared you are, the better your chances for skirting true danger. If you carpool, you should always keep the following items in an easily accessible area of your car: a list of the children's names, ages, genders, and parents' names and addresses; signed and notarized permission slips from parents authorizing medical treatment in the event that they can't be reached; a flashlight and first-aid kit; a cell phone; bottled water; a blanket; and tissues or baby wipes.

You need to do everything in your power to ensure safe carpool trips. Adhere to the rules of the road, and take every safety measure to ensure that every car trip is safe. Maintain a routine when you carpool. Always use the same pickup and drop-off sites. Establish a password for all riders and drivers, so that strangers won't be able to trick kids into getting in their cars. Use seatbelts, car seats, and booster seats for all riders. Never stow backpacks on the floor, where they can get tangled with little feet, or in the rear window, where they can block your vision. Instead, stash them in your trunk. Lastly, remember that foods are considered choking hazards in a moving car because of sudden stops and starts.

Carpooling is serious business — not only are you responsible for your own children's well-being, you are responsible for other children, as well. So the next time you're chauffeuring four six-year-olds to gymnastics, remember that there are hazards lurking at every stoplight. Oh, and remember to have fun, too — some of the best childhood memories are made during carpools!

34.

Mom's Temper Tantrum

Some days, the frustration of being a parent can soar to heights that you never dreamed possible. With children, there is friction, and when friction meets up with your exhaustion—there is inevitably combustion. This is the moment when otherwise good, decent mothers "lose it."

Say it's been a less-than-great day, thanks to your three-year-old daughter's constant demands and crankiness. Your husband arrives home from work and suggests going out to eat. You're relieved—a change of scenery will do you a world of good.

Before leaving, you take your daughter to the bathroom. But she needs to go again right when your food is served, and then three more times during the meal. Of course, this serves to foil the very reason you are out to dinner. You find yourself yelling at her—which you hate to do—out of sheer frustration. This escalates her cranky mood, and she starts kicking your chair, crying, "I want to go now!" You slowly lose your composure, your dignity, your reason, and worst of all, your sense of humor.

When you hit your boiling point—and you will—take a deep breath and try to get past it. Remember that you are your child's teacher, and she must learn how to act kindly and thoughtfully by your example and guidance. If you constantly lose it, she will, too. When your child is pushing your buttons like crazy, consider that attention is really what she's after. Try to avoid a confrontation by suddenly hugging and kissing her.

If you're getting so angry that you scare your child, you're going to need a time-out. Take a moment to cool off—maybe a walk around the restaurant—then calmly explain to your child what you're doing and why.

If all else fails and you find that you're losing your temper and are powerless to stop, create a mantra and repeat it over and over: "Let it go. Let it go. Let it go." Then let it go.

35.

Who's a Stranger?

As much as we try, parents can't keep their eyes on their active children every second of the day. Unfortunately, all it takes is a few seconds for somebody to abduct a child. What we can do, however, is teach our kids everything there is to know about strangers.

Begin by asking your child what he thinks a stranger looks like. Tell him that a stranger is everybody that he has never met before. A stranger could be anyone—a neighbor, a lady on the street, or even somebody from Daddy's office. Also tell your child that strangers can be nice people! Explain that there are nice strangers and mean strangers, and since they can't tell them apart just by looking at them, they should never go anywhere with strangers.

For obvious reasons, we implore our children to never speak to strangers. Many mothers feel that this backfires in situations where they want to also teach their children to be friendly. For example, you take your son to a store. The clerk says, "Hi!" and your son replies, "You're a stranger! Go away!" Before you cringe, realize that your son is doing exactly the right thing. Be proud of him for following the safety rules that you've taught. In time, he'll learn to distinguish between strangers and nice people. You might want to explain that if you're with him and a stranger speaks to him, he can ask you first to see if it's okay to reply.

Reinforce the rules about strangers as often as possible. Many parents talk with their children about the subject once, and then think it's a done deal. This isn't true. As children develop, they process information differently. That's why it's important to update your "strangers" speech every three months or so. This requires extra effort and attention on your part, but the rewards are worth it.

36.

Stepmother Syndrome

Stepmothers seem to take a lot of heat for not doing things that their stepchildren's biological father and mother should do. Though women may often play certain roles in the household—grocery shopper, health consumer, and education advocate, for example—in a home with a stepmother, these roles are often better played by the children's father. But he may not step up to the jobs. In other situations, the children's biological mother doesn't allow the stepmother to do these things for her children.

Another possibility is that a stepmother may not be able to take on these responsibilities. A stepmother may want to take her stepchild to the dentist or to the doctor, but the stepchild might refuse to go with her. In other situations, stepmothers aren't legally permitted to participate in their stepchildren's medical care or education. Stepmothers and stepfathers do not have the legal authority to handle medical situations, deal with schools, or participate in their stepchildren's religious upbringing.

In defense of stepmothers, raising stepchildren is hard work and can be especially difficult when there is no support from the biological mother. In some instances, a stepmother has a closer relationship with her stepchildren than the children have with their biological mother. But often that isn't the case. Many stepmother/stepchild relationships are strained because of animosity toward the stepmother from the biological mother, to whom the child is devoted.

Stepmothers who have successful relationships with their stepchildren can feel proud of the fact they were able to beat the odds. Those who have unfavorable relationships with their stepchildren needn't be hard on themselves—all relationships take time to grow and nurture. A hardworking stepmother who is there unconditionally for her stepchild will eventually reap the rewards of a loving relationship.

37.

Appreciate Your Coach

Your labor coach isn't just there to time your contractions and feed you ice chips. In fact, studies have shown that partners can contribute a lot more than that. Effective labor support can actually shorten labor and prevent complications. A generation ago, expectant fathers stayed in the waiting room while their wives did all the work. But it's been since proven that when Dads were brought into the delivery room, laboring Moms became more relaxed, experienced less pain, and labored more quickly and easily.

That said, you should now have a newfound appreciation for your labor coach. Here are a few more ideas for him so he can be at his best for you.

Make sure Mom is relaxed. Tensing up during a contraction only increases the pain of that contraction. Have her focus on relaxing each part of her body while you massage each of them.

Use a tennis ball to ease back pain. Back labor is the worst! By pressing your fist or a tennis ball firmly below the small of your partner's back, you may be able to relieve some of the pain. Mark the spot on her back with a marker that so you can find it fast.

In addition to massaging tense areas, stroke your partner's skin during contractions. Stroking is a gentler touch than massaging. Stroke the length of her arm, face, and neck. Hair brushing or other light stimulation can reduce pain, as well.

Deal with all of the phone calls and the anxious relatives in the waiting room.

Tell your partner what a great job she is doing. Yes, she may tell you to shut up, but she doesn't really mean that. Just keep on praising.

Enjoy the experience. Labor is very hard work, but seeing the birth of a baby is an experience that you'll never forget!

Your labor coach is ready to go. Good luck, and don't forget to tell him how much you appreciate his help—even if, in the end, all he can manage to do is supply you with ice chips.

38.

Have a Blast with Your Past!

One Saturday night, you'll be cleaning the gunk off of your baby's highchair, and you'll think back to a Saturday night—not long ago—when you were out with your friends, laughing the night away. For a fleeting instant, you'll wish that you were back at that time in your life—before you got pregnant.

But truth be told, you wouldn't trade your new life for anything! Yes, there are messes to be cleaned and a lot of clothes to wash. But you also have a little angel that you didn't have back in your younger days—an angel that has given you more joy and happiness than anything else.

Your life is different now. You have a baby, and along with that baby come new responsibilities and lifestyle changes. But like every new mom, you also have new anxieties, new stress, and new wants and needs. Should one of those desires be to revisit your old life—even for a fleeting few hours—then the best thing you can do for yourself and your family is indulge!

Reverting back to your pre-baby self can be the most invigorating experience you have as a new mother. It's a chance to leave your stress behind and take delight in familiar surroundings and activities. Don't miss out on a night of fun with old friends—even if you're beyond exhaustion. Leave your husband in charge, and enjoy an evening out.

It might surprise you how much this experience can rejuvenate you. You'll be a little more tired, but you'll have the best of both worlds! And going out without your family will give you a chance to miss them a little, too.

39.

Mother/Daughter Time

There's nothing more beautiful than spending the day with your little girl, playing dress-up and house, or singing and dancing to kiddie songs. The gowns, the jewels, the music — it's all a wonderful, integral part of mother/daughter bonding.

However, it's important to share some of that bonding time participating in activities not normally associated with little girl play. Go against stereotypes and offer to play cars, play with a building and construction set, or play sports with your daughter. These activities empower her to be all that she can be, and grow into a well-rounded, well-adjusted young woman.

Typically, though your daughter's playgroups and preschool will offer dual-gender activities, given the option, most little girls migrate to the girl toys, while the boys flock to the boy toys. It's a tough practice to break, since children enjoy playing in group situations with other kids of the same gender. There's nothing wrong with this, except that if these are the only activities your daughter is encouraged to do — in and out of school — she won't get the chance to broaden her horizons. While most boys are busy playing sports or building with blocks, girls often miss out on important developmental skills in these areas.

One of the best things a mother can do for her daughter is to provide an atmosphere where all opportunities are available. Consider planning your time alone with your daughter constructively — perhaps a half-hour of dress-up, followed by a half-hour of blocks. Or a half-hour of dolls followed by a half-hour of soccer. Be daring and buy her a toy truck or a train set for her birthday, to give her other options for play. Your daughter will become comfortable participating in all kinds of activities, and will gain a broader base of hobbies and talents.

We are lucky enough today that women can follow their true interests. Let's make sure we give them a chance to figure out what they are from the very beginning.

40.

Mother/Son Time

Just as it's essential for a mother to spend some time with her daughter breaking the stereotypes associated with girl play, it's important for her to treat her son in the same manner. Not only are boys never encouraged to play with girl toys, they are almost always discouraged from doing so. There are many activities often labeled "for girls" that really aren't. Activities in which your son should be participating can include arts and crafts, playing with dolls, housekeeping, and creative writing.

It's no wonder that new fathers feel like foreigners when it comes to taking care of infants—as kids, they never had the chance to pretend that they were fathers; to nurture and care for baby dolls. These are the fathers that cringe when their sons run straight for the nearest toy vacuum at preschool! It's unfortunate that society creates such stereotypes about playing. If boys were encouraged at a young age to play with dolls or explore toy kitchens, they might fall into fatherhood as easily as many women fall into motherhood. They'd know how to change diapers, run vacuums, and bake cookies.

Moms need to devote some of their daily playtime with their sons to activities that they might not be exposed to at school or in a playgroup situation. Baking, playing house, or even playing dress-up are extremely enjoyable activities for little boys. Choose costumes that are boy-friendly and appropriate. Try buying a wooden dollhouse for your son's next birthday, and you'll be amazed at how much he learns about family dynamics.

Don't forget to encourage his creativity, too. As they grow older, boys are generally pushed toward after-school activities such as sports or science, and are steered away from art and creative writing. But with a little effort, you can engage your son in a more well-rounded selection of activities that include sports as well as art, and science as well as writing.

For now, encourage your son no matter what his interests are. If he's developed a love for books and writing, spend a day with him writing and illustrating stories, or get him hooked on an interesting book series. The possibilities are endless, as long as you're able to look past the stereotypes. Then you can be sure that your boy will grow up to be a well-balanced young man.

41.

Working Mothers

There's no avoiding it—for every new or expectant mother, the question comes up sooner or later: Should I quit my job to stay at home with my baby?

There's no easy answer, and there's no *right* answer either. Research has proven that a mother's decision to work or stay home isn't a good indicator of how her child will turn out—unless, of course, her child's care is substandard. What's more important than whether or not a mother chooses to go back to work is how she feels about her decision. If she's unhappy, her sadness and anger can spill over into her interaction with her kids.

Deciding what's best for your family is no simple task. It helps to start with a rational assessment of the trade-offs you face. Then review your family finances, and be honest with your partner. Think about Social Security and retirement benefits that are based on lifetime earnings. It may not make financial sense for Mom to stay home if her retirement possibilities are financially more beneficial than Dad's.

Discuss with your spouse how life will change around the house with a tighter budget. One-income families often need to make many tough choices about spending—choices they don't always agree on. If there is already a lot of stress in your life, you may not want to add financial stress into the mix.

You'll want to also discuss with your spouse what it means for your career, should you decide not to go back to work. Will you still be marketable years down the road when you re-enter the workplace?

Leaving her job can also affect a woman's self-image and the dynamics of her marriage. Some women who become stay-at-home moms find that they've left a job that they love for a job that they also love, but that includes many things that they hate: cooking, cleaning, and other chores. Feelings of resentment can affect your self-esteem, not to mention your marriage.

One big consideration a new mother faces with regard to working or staying at home is child care. Some women believe that a child needs a parent at home, and they are happy to quit their jobs for that reason alone. Other women feel that baby-sitting or daycare is a wonderful option for their child, should they need to work.

To work, or not to work…that is the question that you'll spend many hours discussing with your spouse. When it seems overwhelming, think about this: At least there are options!

42.

Call Your Mother!

Before you had your first child, you and your spouse surely anticipated that you would have some opposing opinions on how to raise her. Not widely varying opinions, mind you, but slightly different styles of parenting. Now that you have a child, you're learning to work through your differences and come to solutions that you're both comfortable with. Enter Grandma and Grandpa (or two of each), and you suddenly have new sets of opinions demanding to be heard!

There are two types of grandparents. There are grandparents who participate in the modern world of cell phones, computers, and ATM cards, and there are grandparents who are content to keep things as they were a decade or two ago. Before getting into a power struggle with your parents or your husband's parents, decide which category they fit into, and deal with them appropriately.

For example, many grandparents encourage their daughters to return to work after their maternity leaves. Other grandparents firmly believe that a mother should be home with her baby. These grandparents need to be handled differently. Remember that one of the hardest things about being a grandparent is relinquishing control. Grandparents who are stuck in yesteryear remember having total control over raising their children. When it comes to raising *your* children, they understand that they are not in charge anymore, but may find it difficult to bite their tongues.

You and your parents may never agree on when to take the pacifier away from your daughter, or when to potty train her, or how long she must wait after dinner before having a cookie, but don't be angry at your parents for trying. You need to be patient and keep their remarks from bothering you. And they need to learn self-control when it comes to shelling out parenting advice.

The importance of a good grandparent/grandchild relationship outweighs everything else. There's nothing more heartwarming than seeing your daughter's face light up every time Grandma and Grandpa come through the door. The next time they do pay a visit, make it a point of showing them how happy your daughter is and how she's thriving beautifully. Then tell them, "The proof is in the pudding! I'm obviously doing something right!"

43.

Learn the Routine

Regular schedules provide a framework that puts order into a young child's world. Predictability can be tedious for adults, but children thrive on it! Sameness, repetition, and knowing what to expect help children become more confident.

Routines begin right away when a baby is born, and help set the stage for easier days and nights as your child grows older. Babies especially need regular sleep and meal schedules—they even need the routines that lead up to those activities, such as a story before bed, or going to a certain chair for a feeding. It's amazing how an infant can learn that when Mommy carries him into her bedroom, he's about to be fed.

The first step in creating a routine is choosing the activities you want to accomplish. The next step is simply following that routine exactly the same way each time! By doing so, you're establishing a pattern in your baby's life—one that he becomes familiar with over time. As he grows older, knowing what is going to happen when and who is going to be there allows him to feel more comfortable.

Be consistent. If you're trying to get your preschooler in a mealtime routine, sit together at the dinner table every night (if that's what works for you), and share your experiences from the day. Sit in the same chairs and try to eat at the same time every evening. Mealtime is also the perfect time to introduce him to other routines, such as cleaning up the playroom beforehand and setting and clearing the table—routines which give children a sense of responsibility.

Before bedtime, consistent nightly rituals are most soothing for children. Give yourself a good half-hour of downtime with your child—incorporate it into the routine—before brushing teeth, reading a story, and tucking him in. Find out what works best for your child. Maybe he likes listening to music instead of hearing a story. Or maybe he needs three kisses on the head before he can comfortably surrender to sleep. Whatever his needs, together you can construct the perfect routine!

44.

A Soccer Mom Story

The list of activities that children pursue these days is staggering: sports, art, music, dance, theater... Shuttling them around monopolizes your after-school and weekend hours. Parental fatigue aside, you can't help but wonder if it all isn't a bit much. A few years ago, studies supported the idea that we were overscheduling our kids and placing undue stress on them. But today, reports have confirmed that children not only have more free time despite the running around, but that their free time is more structured.

Children today have more opportunity to explore their world by participating in many different activities. According to the study, kids are now spending much less time in front of the TV, more time on homework, and more time helping with chores and errands.

Think back to the activities you were involved in as a kid. You may have had a sport or music lesson here and there, but it's a good bet that you spent many after-school afternoons playing tag outdoors, listening to music, or watching reruns of old TV shows. Your kids are doing the same (hopefully minus the TV)—they're just doing it all with better supervision and in a more organized atmosphere.

While it's certainly possible to overdo it, all of those sports and classes and lessons can be good for children. Today's kids have the chance to grow up exposed to a wider range of athletics and creative arts than any previous generation. And with more girls' organized sports available, girls today have many more opportunities in sports.

We all want our children to be challenged and happy. We want them to learn such lifelong skills as teamwork and goal-setting. We need to recognize that while chauffeuring our kids around town to various activities may be exhausting for us, without these activities, our kids might end up watching TV or playing video games.

45.

Disciplining Your Kids

Moms studying the art of discipline must remember the two cardinal rules: One is, "Don't waste your breath." With a young child, it's all about being in control. Resist the urge to get caught up in a long battle of "Why?" Tell your child what you want done, why you want it done, and how. Tell her once, and then move on to reprimanding her when she doesn't oblige.

There are four steps to effectively communicating what you want, and most kids will "get it" if you offer them all four steps. Leave one out, and you're setting yourself up for trouble. Begin with asking your child to do (or not do) something: "No eating in the family room." Offer an explanation: "The food gets on the floor, and we'll get bugs in the house." Present the consequences: "If you continue to eat in the family room, I'll have to take your snack away." And finally, give an alternative: "Why don't we tape the show you're watching so that you don't miss it while you eat your snack in the kitchen?"

Ready for the second rule? The second rule is, "Always be consistent." The moment that you give in, your children learn that you *will* give in. Stick to your convictions, and steer clear of self-doubt. If you think, "Maybe she's right. Why shouldn't I let her have one more cookie?" you're starting to waver! Even if it really isn't so bad if she has another cookie, once you say no, follow through. Reversing yourself only shows that you're malleable, and sends your child the message that if she cries, whines, or protests enough, you'll change your mind.

Discipline can be incredibly tricky. The best advice is to try different discipline styles, and then pick the one that works best for you.

46.

Mom's Home Spa

Every hardworking mother deserves a week at a spa. But with the high cost of spas these days, that same hardworking Mom will need to sell her firstborn just to pay for it! There is another way, however. Consider treating yourself to a mini-spa, right in your very own home.

Begin your mini-spa with a yoga-type exercise. Lie flat on your stomach, and bring yourself up onto your elbows and knees, keeping your legs bent. Your elbows should be in line with your shoulders. Create a straight line from your ears and shoulders to your hips and knees. Tighten and lift your abdomen, trying to avoid arching your back. Count to fifteen, breathing normally, and then rest. Three sets of this will help tighten your stomach muscles and work your shoulders and hips, too.

Next, head for the shower! A good shower can be as relaxing and revitalizing as a leisurely bath. Create an inviting space in your bathroom, with soft lighting, fragrant candles, or a sprig of eucalyptus hanging from the curtain rod. (The steam from the shower will release the herb's aroma.) Play your favorite mellow CD. The water should be set to a moderately warm temperature and the shower head adjusted to the most powerful setting. Let the water massage your shoulders, spine, and lower back, and then lift each foot separately into the stream.

As you wash your hair, concentrate on massaging your scalp and focus on how it feels. Don't think about what the baby is doing, or what you're going to make for dinner that night. This is time for just you. Finish your shower massage with a thirty-second rinse. Use cool water if you need to invigorate, or warm water if you need to stay relaxed.

The experts say that after a rejuvenating shower, it's best to treat yourself to a healthy, well-balanced meal—like a veggie pizza or a wrap. But if you want to really treat yourself, grab a scoop of ice cream, and dig in!

47.

Interview with a Baby-Sitter

While no one can replace a parent's love and care, a competent, caring, temporary caregiver can be found with time, research, and a lot of patience. If you're one of those mothers who insists that her children are better off never being left with a sitter, you're wrong. Baby-sitters—especially teenagers—can add a new dimension to the relationships your young children have with others. With baby-sitters, they get instant grown-up friends whom they wouldn't ordinarily have interaction with. A great sitter will teach your five-year-old daughter all the new dance steps, or play video games with your eight-year-old son to his heart's content. You owe it to them, to your marriage, and to yourself to take an occasional night "off duty" and hire a sitter.

Begin your search for a baby-sitter with recommendations from friends, neighbors, or coworkers. If that falls flat, contact your church, synagogue, or community center—many offer a baby-sitter training course and provide families with a list of graduates.

When you ask a potential baby-sitter to come by for an interview, pay close attention to how he or she interacts with your kids. Watch for clues that indicate a relaxed, natural rapport, and see if the potential sitter gets down to their level for play. Inattention, overactivity, or preoccupation may be signs of immaturity. Include the following questions in your interview.

Have you cared for children in the past? How old were they? What fun activities do you like to do with the children that you sit for? What would you do if our child cried after we left? What would you do if he refused to go to bed?

Ask your sitter if he or she is trained in CPR or first aid, and discuss the proper procedure for common childhood accidents. Remember that most baby-sitters are inexperienced and unprepared for child-care emergencies. This doesn't make them ineligible to care for your kids. When you find a baby-sitter who is warm, competent and friendly, insist that he or she complete a baby-sitter training course, or spend time guiding and teaching the sitter before leaving him or her alone with your child. Above all, before you step foot from your house for a night out, check your sitter's references. Call families who have used the sitter before.

Take the necessary precautions. You can find a sitter who will take great care of your kids, and develop lasting, loving relationships with them in the process!

48.

Mom to Be

The moment a woman learns that she is pregnant is the moment that she becomes a mother. Though it may not feel like it, by taking care of herself during pregnancy—regularly visiting an obstetrician and making the right choices regarding diet and exercise—a pregnant woman has already begun the responsibilities of motherhood.

Long before you even become pregnant, you'll begin thinking about how having a family will change your approach to life. You and your partner may have very different ideas about how to raise a child, not to mention different opinions about how and where you want the birth of your first child to take place. You should examine your own attitudes and beliefs about parenthood and birth—ideas that hopefully you will discuss with your partner. This type of preparation is what being a parent is all about. Though you may not yet have that tiny treasure in your arms, you're already thinking about the child's welfare and loving the baby unconditionally.

The best thing you can do for your unborn baby is to make sure that you take the time to baby yourself a little, too! It's believed that men and women who have felt nurtured in their lives make the most nurturing parents. You'll be a better parent if you're loving and gentle toward yourself during your pregnancy. Notice the things that make you feel good—long walks alone or with your partner, going to lunch with friends, singing out loud—whatever! Recognize that you are a very important person, and though the focus of others may be that bulging belly of yours, you should learn to focus on yourself.

Should Mother's Day come while you're pregnant, celebrate the day with pride and festivity! For some, this day is a rite of passage. For others, it's a joyful celebration after a struggle with infertility. Whether you're already a mom or you're a mom-to-be, Mother's Day is *your* day. Enjoy it!

49.

Be a Breadwinner, Too

For some mothers—especially moms who left their jobs after the baby was born—the desire to return to work frequently surfaces during their child's first year. They crave that interaction with coworkers, the constant intellectual stimulation, and the paycheck at the end of the week! As for mothers who didn't work before having their babies, they, too, crave outside stimuli because (and it's okay to admit this) they're bored!

The answer: part-time work! Part-time work offers the best of both worlds, and should you find adequate child care, you'd be silly not to pursue it. For many, it's the perfect balance—working one, two, or three days a week and caring for your child the other four, five, or six.

You may want to begin your job search by revisiting your old office and treating your former boss to lunch. Explain that you are available for work on a part-time basis, and can set up a home office if need be. Many companies often fail to replace women who depart on maternity leave. Learning more about the situation in your old office may prove to be very beneficial.

Or perhaps you're looking for something completely different from your former career. There are plenty of home businesses that can be fruitful and fun. Let's say you've turned out to be the best mom ever; a mother who loves every second of child play and care. You might want to think about providing daycare in your home. Often, this is a perfect setup for a mother of one—she can still give her child needed attention and care for another in the process. Her little one can also make a new friend. Child care is a very profitable service—there is never a shortage of families looking for excellent care for their kids.

Another way you can earn extra money—and in some cases *a lot* of it—is by teaching. Academia offers great job opportunities for new mothers. Not only does a teaching position offer workplace flexibility, but it's a good way to keep on top of what's happening in your field. Though working as a part-time instructor, you aren't entitled to certain benefits, these positions are excellent options for non-accredited teachers looking to venture back into the working world. In addition to private schools and community colleges, part-time teaching options can also be found at your local dance studios, exercise clubs, and community centers.

The bottom line is that you shouldn't limit yourself. If you're interested in making changes, earning money, or *both*, you need to explore your options.

50.

Your Home Office

Working at home may seem like the perfect way to balance job and family. There's no commute, no colleagues popping into your office to chat, and no reason to fork over big bucks for lunch every day. Just uninterrupted blocks of time to get your work done, right?

Not necessarily. If you're prone to distractions, or if you have trouble motivating yourself in the morning, working at home isn't your best choice. People don't realize the amount of discipline needed to make working at home successful. Should you still be committed to working part-time, it may pay for you to rent space somewhere else in order to get your work done. Some people rent out separate office space in their homes, or you can consider sharing office space with other working moms.

Believe it or not, the worst distraction in the home office is the telephone. Many friends won't understand that even though you are home, you are working. You can lose *hours* of productive work time answering the telephone during the day. The solution? Get caller ID.

Your husband, too, may take time getting used to your new work situation, so it's imperative that you go over all household chores and errands beforehand and figure out who can handle what.

The two worst distractions that sabotage working at home are television and the stocked refrigerator. Make sure that your office is far enough from the TV that you won't be tempted to turn it on. If you take a break, go for a walk or read the newspaper instead. As for food, it can be tough not to snack nonstop while you sit at a desk for hours, so try setting a timer to go off every hour. When it does, treat yourself to a stretch and a small snack. Always keep a bottle of water at your desk.

Some experts estimate that one out of every five home-office setups fails because people don't realize the amount of cooperation needed to make it work successfully. Prepare yourself and your family before you begin, and understand that your work time is just as valuable as your partner's! Most of all, remember that working at home is supposed to make your life easier—not harder!

51.

Go Ask Your Father!

Does this sound like a familiar scenario? Dad is in the kitchen with the kids. Mom is upstairs in the shower. The kids want a snack, but instead of just asking Dad, your little angels walk halfway across the house and interrupt your fifteen minutes of private time to ask you to get them something to eat!

Why does this happen? It's enough to send any mother into a frenzy of frustration. Unfortunately, the blame in this case often lies with the mother. She has created an atmosphere at home where she is constantly the parent that meets the demands of her kids. Perhaps in her inability to give up control, she doesn't let Dad do anything for the kids.

Dads are not completely blameless, however—they let this happen! Mothers and fathers need to make shared parenting their goal. Mom needs to let go of some control—to trust that if she leaves the kids with Dad, they won't starve. Dads, for their part, need to become more secure in their roles. They need to work at improving their talents at multitasking—juggling grocery lists, office work, and doctor's appointments all at the same time. Dads must also actively search out ways to do their full share. They need to learn to anticipate their children's needs.

Paying attention to your kids is where it all starts. Moms—if they are home with their children—learn how to do this from day one. Dads usually have evenings and weekends to figure it out. For this reason, mothers need to take a step to the side and let fathers parent the kids for long stretches of time. It will give Dad the experience he needs, and give your kids time to adjust to the way their father does things.

Eventually, it will make a huge difference in your life. Your kids will get used to asking Dad for help, and you may even get some uninterrupted time in the bathroom.

52.

Excursions for Preschoolers

How many times can you go to the park? Or the playground? Or the nearest fast-food joint? Sometimes, it's easy to get stuck in a boring routine with your child, going to the same park, the same playground, and then out for pizza or fast food every day for lunch.

With a little extra effort, you can find more exciting, interesting excursions to take with your preschooler, no matter where you live. There are many outings that will enrich your child's mind, fulfill his need for physical activity, and just be plain fun!

Start with the nearest petting zoo. Kids love playing with the animals, and learn a lot about farms in the process. Museums make great sites for preschoolers' play dates, too. There are children's museums all across the country that offer age-appropriate experiments, hands-on activities, art classes, and music lessons for young children in the morning hours. Since most have cafeterias, you can often stay through lunch.

Short, simple trips are perfect opportunities to teach children about how things work away from home. Consider paying a visit to your local fire department. Bring along a book about firefighters, some toy fire trucks, and some crayons and paper for your child to illustrate his experiences. If you're lucky, a firefighter can show your child around and explain how the equipment is used.

Many parents love taking their children to the airport to watch planes take off and land. Make sure to visit a small airport with your child to avoid crowds and difficult parking situations. Construction sites, the police station, hospitals, farmers' markets, libraries, and animal shelters also make excellent places for preschoolers to explore. Until his first visit, all your child will know about these places will come from books or through television. Visiting each place in person and having professionals explain their functions and answer questions can be one of the most rewarding experiences your preschooler can have.

53.

"Mommy, I Love You!"

There are no other words more heartwarming to hear than, "Mommy, I love you." Nothing can compare to hearing your child first profess her love!

At around nine months, when your child's motor skills and coordination are better developed, she will begin to embrace people, pets, and other things like blankets and stuffed animals. And though she adores you like crazy, her actions at this point aren't true signs of affection. Babies simply love to imitate, and may mirror kisses by touching their lips to your face.

A few months down the road, however, your baby will learn to understand that there are names for what she's doing. When prompted to "give Mommy a kiss good-night," she'll gladly play the game and oblige. Finally, by eighteen months (or sooner), she'll realize that hugs and kisses are ways to demonstrate love. At that point, she won't need much encouragement from you!

Still, there may come a day when your little beloved refuses to give you a kiss. It will break your heart, for sure, but don't let it upset you. Kids want and need affection, but toddlers, preschoolers, and elementary-age kids may rebuff it in order to express their independence. Remember that it's most likely just a phase she's going through, and eventually she'll return to her old lovable self.

Some kids run hot and cold when it comes to affection. Your daughter may reject your kisses in the morning, and then ask you for kisses in the afternoon. Never refuse kisses and hugs as "payback"—it could lead your child to believe that you don't love her anymore.

It's important to remember that kids—especially six years and older—worry what their friends will think of them. They want to appear mature and independent at all times, and kisses from Mommy can compromise their independence. Keep in mind that your child still loves you like crazy. She just may be saving her loving, cuddly nature for the privacy of home!

54.

School at Home

Home schooling is a growing trend, quietly gaining momentum in every state. And home-schooled kids are being taken seriously by the outside academic world more than ever before. In fact, research shows that sixty-nine percent of all home-schoolers go on to college or other higher-learning institutions.

With test scores on a national decline in public schools, more parents are choosing to home-school their kids. But before you quit your job as an advertising exec to become your children's full-time teacher, do your homework: There are both pros and cons to home schooling.

Two questions you may want to ask yourself are: Do parents make the best teachers? And can any child succeed at home schooling? It's important to explore the answers to both before making such a vital decision.

By choosing home schooling, parents have 100 percent involvement in their children's education, and under most circumstances, follow an approved curriculum developed by child educators. They can monitor their children's progress on a daily basis, choose a structure together with their kids that works best for them, and progress at their own rate.

This approach to education, though it may sound glamorous, is met by a lot of criticism. Some researchers believe that home-schooled children are limited to their parents' notions and ideas of what's proper and acceptable, and ultimately become no further educated than their parents. Above all, they believe children need school for their social development.

However, studies have shown that home-schooled kids actually behave better in group situations. In addition, many neighborhood library and sports programs have begun to offer classes for home-schooled kids during the day, hoping to provide more social situations for them.

If you're seriously considering home schooling, you may be part of the growing number of parents frustrated by their school systems. Look for conferences on home schooling, or join a support group in your area. Ask yourself if you like staying home with your children, and if you have a good balance between home and work. Most importantly, are you willing to put your career on hold to home-school? A lot of parents burn out trying to be the perfect teacher to their kids, but home schooling, done with humor, patience, a sense of purpose, and a thirst for knowledge can be a joyful experience for both you and your children!

55.

Some Peace and Quiet

Our busy schedules, combined with our kids' natural rhythms, conspire to turn the hours before and during dinner into the most hectic part of the day. With careful preparation and strategic planning, you can make this a time to connect rather than a time to self-destruct!

First, distinguish the events that lead up to dinner. The end of the day is typically a time for low physical energy. The trouble is that we can't rest because there's too much to be done — homework to finish, meals to prepare, diapers to be changed, kids' fighting to stop, and the inevitable phone calls to answer. Children are making the transition from daycare or school to home at this time, and they need our attention. When we don't provide it, they only get more clingy and unreasonable.

Allow yourself to unwind before facing this daily period. If you're a working mom, use your commute home to collect yourself. When you arrive home, change into comfortable clothes before doing anything else.

Before you begin to prepare dinner, give your kids your undivided attention—maybe fifteen minutes of snuggling on the couch or coloring together. When your children don't get your attention, they become even more demanding, so beat them to the punch.

Many times, your family's evening edginess is due to hunger. Keep pre-dinner snacks on hand and serve them immediately. Cut-up vegetables and dip, cheese and crackers—serve anything healthy that can help take the edge of hunger off.

Letting your child watch TV can add chaos to an already frenzied home atmosphere. The background noise can make you more tense, and you'll need to raise your voice in order to talk to your child. Instead, have a box of art supplies on hand for making pre-dinner masterpieces. Then keep dinner simple. Weeknights are not an ideal time to try new or complicated recipes.

Keep your cool and hang in there! After dinner, your child's natural rhythms are slowing him down, getting him ready for sleep. Once fed, you can end the evening with his usual bedtime routine.

56.

Health-Conscious Kids

Raising health-conscious kids seems harder than ever. Many years ago, children ate whatever was fresh and seasonal—there weren't as many choices as we have now. Readily available processed foods provide zero nutrition so that our children miss out on eating nutritionally rich foods. Nutritionally speaking, progress is taking us backward.

Your choices are what ultimately will determine if your children will grow up to be health-conscious. If your snack drawer and refrigerator are always stocked with junk food, that's going to be the norm for your kids. In addition to weight problems, there's a good chance that children with frequent access to these foods will experience low energy, learning difficulties, and dental problems in the not-so-distant future.

Make it a point to control what your kids eat—at least what they eat at home. Once they get to public school, you'll find that you have little or no control over what they eat in class parties, school cafeterias, friend's homes, or after-school programs. Reconstruct your refrigerator to include healthier choices, like whole-wheat or whole-grain bread instead of white, frozen yogurt instead of ice cream, and any and all fruits and veggies that your children like. Make sure you always have ice-cold water on hand, and resist the urge to bring candy into the house. Save it for special times only.

In the pantry, offer pretzels, popcorn, and rice cakes over fatty, fried potato and corn chips. Buy cereals containing less than ten grams of sugar rather than sugar-packed cereals.

Set a healthy example for your children. You can be sure that they will thank you for it when they're older!

57.

Your Daughter's Self-Image

Young children regard their bodies with a happy lack of self-consciousness. At age three and four, children are content with the way that they look. By age five, children take more interest in their appearances—girls especially. They are more careful of how they wear their hair or the clothes they choose to wear. But somewhere around age six or seven, something happens to our kids—they become self-conscious of their bodies and may even want privacy from their own mother.

How does it happen? There are many reasons that a child can suddenly become aware of her weight or how she looks—perhaps a classmate has made a cruel remark, or maybe the media has had an influence on her. There are, in fact, a large percentage of mothers who unknowingly fuel this insecurity. They can't look at their daughters in bathing suits without cause for concern.

Experts say that the anguish these mothers are feeling is related to their beliefs about their own bodies. In some cases, a mother may have been overweight as a child and doesn't want her daughter to experience that. Regardless, it's a lot of pressure to put on a little girl.

Pediatricians implore concerned mothers to realize that girls between the ages of nine and twelve go through many changes as their bodies prepare for the growth spurt that lies ahead. Many mothers mistake this extra weight—as little as it may be—as a sign that their daughter is getting fat. Instead, doctors urge, it's essential for a mother to exude positive messages to her daughter, especially where weight and nutrition are concerned. Remind her that successful, happy, attractive people come in all sizes and shapes. Talk to her about media images and how TV, magazines, advertisers, and movies all aim to make actors and actresses look better than they normally do with special effects and makeup.

Certainly, there are mothers who do have cause for concern—childhood obesity is a major problem in this country. But if your prepubescent daughter falls within her recommended height and weight on the charts, and she's leading a healthy, active lifestyle, avoid putting any doubt in her mind about how much she's eating or the way that she looks.

Above all, tell your daughter that it makes you proud to see her growing up, and continue to encourage her with positive messages. Tell her that she's beautiful—it's something that you can never say too many times!

58.

Your Child, the Teacher, and You

There's a lot a parent can do to establish wonderful relationships between parent and teacher and teacher and child. A strong relationship creates a better climate for learning, and improves the odds that your child will excel.

Be involved. Your involvement signals to the teacher and your child that you value what's happening in class. If you skip events and never ask about activities, you're sending the message that you don't care. No matter how busy your schedule is, make it to parents' night at school and introduce yourself. If possible, sign up for something—whether it's to bring cupcakes for a holiday party or read a book to the class during story time.

Prepare your child for school—every single day. Make sure he always has the right supplies and enough of them, check up on his homework, keep abreast of his projects, and send back permission slips and other correspondence on time.

Keep in touch with your child's teacher. Schedule conferences if you have concerns, or call to discuss anything that has to do with your child's education. There may be things going on in the classroom that change your child's behavior at home. His teacher may have insight into why this is happening. This works both ways, too: The more a teacher knows about your family, the better the teacher will be able to connect with your child. Keep the teacher posted if a big change occurs in your family—the death of a pet or a relative or a potential divorce. Parents are often reluctant to reveal personal matters, but when there is stress in the family, it always spills over into a child's school performance.

What's the best way to win points with your child's teachers? Give positive feedback on their performance. Send in a note of praise, a thank-you for recommending a good book for your child, a holiday card—anything that will show teachers that you're appreciative of their effort.

59.

How to Tell Your Boss

When your pregnancy is officially confirmed, it's a time to rejoice, a time to plan, a time to tell your parents, in-laws, family, and friends—and a time to tell your boss. Talk about stress! Breaking the news about pregnancy to the boss is thought to be one of the most agonizing things a working woman will come across in her life. And she has good reason to worry—many women who announce their pregnancies at the office often experience an immediate change in their office atmospheres. They're suddenly treated differently by their bosses. Their workload suddenly lessens. There's always the fear that their maternity leave will become a permanent leave.

Luckily, the law is on the side of expectant moms—in the United States, protections are extensive for pregnant working women, including a guarantee of job reinstatement. If you work for a company with at least fifty employees, you are protected by the Family Medical Leave Act and guaranteed twelve weeks maternity leave (after twelve months of employment). Many larger companies may offer a percentage of earned wages during maternity leave and continue health, life, and other benefits. You are also guaranteed the same or similar job of comparable pay and responsibilities when you return. If your company has at least fifteen employees, you're covered under the Pregnancy Discrimination Act, which states that an employer must treat pregnant women the same as other employees with non-pregnancy disabilities.

The best thing that you can do before you let the cat out of the bag at work is be prepared! Learn about the law in your state, and know your rights and obligations. Do a little investigative work around the office—check out your company's maternity leave policies, and talk in confidence to some coworker moms to find out how management reacted in the past to pregnancy announcements.

When you're ready to make your announcement, be sure that your boss is ready to *receive* your announcement! Be sensitive to the moods in your office—perhaps pick a time when there is less stress in the picture, such as after a successful meeting, a big sale, or a celebration. Most importantly, do it in person, in private, and have it in writing so that it's properly documented. Employers appreciate employees letting them know early. They feel that it demonstrates a level of professionalism and commitment. Above all, make sure that the news comes from you—not from a coworker!

Try to keep your worrying to a minimum. In this day and age, women are highly regarded in the workplace—companies realize that it will be tough to keep women at all levels if they treat their female employees unfairly.

60.

Class Mothers with Class

Like many moms, you may sometimes find yourself bending over backward to contribute to your child's school. And the fact of the matter is that schools desperately need and appreciate all of the volunteers that they can get! Studies show that children do better academically and behaviorally when their parents get involved in their school. But a recent nationwide survey conducted by the National PTA showed that a majority of parents who want to help out and can't, feel guilty.

One solution for mothers who find themselves in this position is for them to help out on a smaller scale. Sign up for only the committees that give you the most bang for the buck. The rewards are plentiful—you'll develop a relationship with your child's teacher, you'll get to see your child in action in the classroom, you'll network with other parents, and you'll be enhancing your child's education in the process.

For the working mother, class parent responsibilities become overwhelming, as she tries to do too much for the school and work nine to five, as well. Before accepting any task—and this goes for stay-at-home mothers with younger siblings to care for—determine if it's manageable or overwhelming. Try to select jobs that will use your skills and resources.

If you have no time at all to volunteer, the important thing is not to stress over it and feel guilty. Do other things for your child's class that will surely be welcome—donate books or decorations, or send in snacks for class parties.

Perhaps the simplest, most obvious way to be a useful volunteer is to choose an activity that you love doing. Even taking the time to visit your child's class once every few months to read a story can bring you and your child enormous satisfaction.

61.

Surviving the Supermarket

The first rule of thumb in shopping with a toddler or preschooler is this: Don't do it if you don't have to do it. That said, if you're still inclined to shop with your child, there are a few steps that you can take to minimize the damage.

As soon as your child can walk, he'll want out of the wagon. Try to keep him in it as long as humanly possible—stock up on snacks, juice, small toys, and books—and leave them on the seat within reach. You may want to bring specially-designed-for-the-supermarket baby toys—they come with a strap you can use to secure the toy to the wagon. This will limit the frustration of having to pick up a squeaky toy hundreds of times during the course of a shopping trip.

If your little one absolutely has to get out, put him to work! Point to the items you want to buy, and ask him to get each one for you. It will take a lot more time to get through the aisles, but boy, will he be happy.

With older children, a supermarket visit can be equally as harrowing. Establish rules well before walking through the supermarket doors. No fighting, no teasing, no hurting, no touching, and no asking for candy.

The best method for ensuring a rewarding grocery shopping experience is to only bring children with you that have been fed, are not tired, have something to occupy their time with, and have already gone to the bathroom. There's nothing more frustrating than having to wheel a full wagon from one end of a superstore to the only bathroom, which is way over at the other end.

If all else fails, let him bring a handheld video game to play while you shop. If you don't own one, consider buying one for the purpose of supermarket shopping only!

62.

Embrace Your Stress

The hardest part about being a mother is that you never get a break. You never experience downtime anymore. Once you have children, they're always around. They follow you into the bathroom, demand to come with you to get the mail, and always have to tell you something really, really important when you're on the phone.

How do we cope when every aspect of our world has changed? Simple. Embrace your stress! Acknowledge that it's going to happen, and expect it every single day. First off, you'll be pleased when you actually have a stress-free day, and second, you'll reduce all that anxiety!

Accepting that some situations with your kids are going to be extremely stressful actually reduces the amount of stress you're feeling. Say you're worried about having to take your son to the pediatrician. Before you go, prepare yourself. Write down all of the questions for the doctor beforehand, and pack a pencil and paper to record medication dosages.

At home, when things get hectic, it's important to establish some Mommy space — part of the house that you can call your own, where you can embrace your stress and then combat it. Even if the space is in a converted closet, as long as it's off limits to everyone else, it'll work for you. Make time each week to retreat to your Mommy space — for catching up on phone calls, reading, or meditating.

A mom can feel trapped when her world is filled with kid-centered errands and concerns. For this reason, it can do a world of good to get away from anything relating to your children — at least once a week. Join a charity or organization that helps the less fortunate and devote one night a week toward helping others. It will help you put the minor annoyances of your life into perspective.

Remembering to refuel is what finding time and space for oneself is all about. Time away from your children will only serve to benefit your interactions when you are with them.

63.

The Never-Ending Diet

When it comes to teaching good nutrition, actions speak louder than words. Parents (mostly moms) make many mistakes in how they deal with food in front of their children. The first is being obsessed about fat. It may be bad for our diets, but it's an important part of a child's diet—especially a growing child. When it comes to fatty foods and treats, stress moderation rather than deprivation.

Dieting mothers should never put their children on a "diet" without first discussing it with their pediatricians. While many children are overweight in this country, parents—burdened by their own insecurities—often aren't good judges with regard to a normal, healthy weight for their children.

Many moms skip breakfast, and that's a mistake. Kids notice this and figure that it's okay to leave the house without eating. But the morning meal is one of the most important meals for a child. In fact, studies indicate that kids perform better in school when they eat breakfast.

Another faux pas many mothers make is providing soda as a beverage for their kids. Soda has no nutritional value, is loaded with caffeine, and can add unwanted calories to your child's diet. Caffeine-free soda is okay—but limit it to when you eat out of the house, and don't keep it in your fridge.

We often find the need to tell our children what foods we didn't like to eat as kids. When we do this, however, we're discouraging our children from trying things for themselves. We should always encourage our kids to try unfamiliar foods—especially when they're toddlers, who will stick almost anything in their mouths. If we introduce new tastes early on, our kids may be more likely to develop tastes for different foods as they get older.

Remember that you, as Mom, have complete control over what gets stocked in your fridge and pantry. You're most likely the one who does the grocery shopping and the one who prepares the food! So set an example for your kids by offering them only healthy, wholesome foods.

64.

The Dot-Com Mom

The Internet has made mothering far easier than it was twenty or even ten years ago. Where else can you find a cure for your baby's croup within minutes? Or figure out how to assemble your daughter's new dollhouse on Christmas Eve? Or chat with other moms for baby-sitter advice, tips on breastfeeding, and where to buy the most inexpensive diapers—all in the wee hours of the morning? It's all there, right at your fingertips, and right in your own home.

But as fabulous as it is, the upside to the World Wide Web— being loaded with information—is also its greatest drawback. Type "weaning" into your search engine, and you'll discover that there are over 600 sites about weaning. Who has time to plow through 600 sites? New mothers especially don't have the time to conduct complicated searches. If you're looking for help on the Web and come across more information than you bargained for, you're probably better off paying a visit to one large parenting site and locating the information that you need within its pages.

Some mothers do their birthday gift shopping online. Others purchase their pharmacy needs and groceries through the Internet. Still others make use of this technology by paying bills online or keeping in touch with faraway family members via e-mail. If you're not taking advantage of all that the Internet has to offer—if you're not even computer literate—now that you're a mother, it's time that you pushed your fears aside and got clicking. Some schools offer night classes on surfing the Internet—or you might just connect to an Internet provider such as AOL or Yahoo and let their customer service representatives talk you through it.

Don't wait another minute! There's a whole World Wide Web of mothers out there—and some of them are waiting for your advice!

65.

Let Them Help Set the Table

We don't think twice about asking our spouses, our parents, or even our neighbors for help when it's needed. Often, we're so caught up in our needs that we miss the fact that there are a couple of able bodies and a few pairs of extra hands right at our disposal.

Having your children help out around the house is beneficial in many ways. It helps you get your work completed, but it also makes them feel like contributing members of the household, and it enables them to develop a lifelong behavior of being helpful and compassionate toward others. Research shows that children who are taught this behavior at home are less likely to join gangs, and are more able to resist peer pressure as they get older.

Encouraging your children to help and think about others also enhances their own self-esteem. Fostering helpful behavior allows them to relate to others by realizing that they aren't the only ones in the world with needs.

But how much help can little kids really give us? Not much, to be honest! But sometimes, just enough to help you get the job done and just enough to keep them busy so that they don't begin whining.

For example, a two-year-old can help load and unload clothing from the washer and dryer and assist in putting her clean clothes away. In the kitchen, young children love to help set the table and prepare meals, but be forewarned: Enlisting their help with cooking and baking may mean more work for you in the end. When you request help from your kids, be sure that the task you assign your child is age-appropriate and developmentally appropriate. Also, watch that the job you assign is small enough for your child to accomplish. Not being able to complete a task can actually undermine her self-esteem.

Remember to praise your children for the help they give—even if it somehow created more work for you! Focus on what your child did by telling her, "What a good helper you are!" Kids thrive on positive reinforcement.

Older children can reap the benefits from helping around the house, as well. Cleaning, vacuuming, and walking the dog are all ways that children five and older can do their share. They also need praise and positive reinforcement, so be sure to let them know what a good job they have done.

66.

"Mommy…Mommy…Mommy!"

Why do our children interrupt us? Mostly, because they are too young to fully understand what interrupting is. Preschoolers don't understand someone else's point of view or what being rude means, so when they interrupt your conversations, they don't realize that they're doing something wrong. Older children may understand that they're being rude by interrupting, but they haven't yet developed patience to wait for your attention.

We need to help our children tame their interrupting impulses. Explain to them that sometimes Mommy or Daddy will have conversations that don't include them. In order to do this, we must be clear with our expectations—the toughest part for your child will be learning to tell when it's okay to break into your conversation and when it's not. Start by telling him right up front, "I'm going to talk on the phone right now. This is one of those times when you shouldn't interrupt me."

If you plan ahead for situations where you want to engage in a conversation without being interrupted, keep an activity nearby—

one that your child can do without your help—maybe in your pocketbook or by the phone.

The most frustrating interruptions happen during a playgroup situation, at the playground, or at somebody else's home. You're torn between wanting to spend time with your child and wanting to talk to the other mothers. So tell your child that when you first arrive at the playgroup, you're going to play with him for a while. Then you're going to talk to the other moms for a while.

The best place to develop your child's patience skills is during dinnertime at the table. You can stress the importance of being a good listener and giving time to let others have their say. If everyone is given a chance to speak—even the littlest baby—your children will learn that they are important and that you value what they have to say.

67.

Your New Little Roomie

New parents always insist that their home will never succumb to a primary-colored mass of baby toys and accessories. If you're one of those parents, you had better brace yourself for the inevitable. As soon as your baby is born, your home is going to go the way of all the homes across the world that have new babies. Once the baby gifts begin to arrive, you'll gaze around your red, yellow, green, and blue eyesore of a living room and wonder what it used to look like. But aside from the aesthetic changes to your home, some changes are an absolute must upon your baby's arrival.

Keep drapery and blind cords out of reach from the crib and changing table. Install a smoke detector in or near your baby's room. Make sure your windows have window guards, and never place a crib, playpen, or other children's furniture near a window. Plug up all electrical outlets, make sure all toy boxes and chests can't trap a child inside, and never hang toys, crib gyms, or decorations in the crib when your baby can get up on her hands and knees.

Safety is your first priority for your new addition—more important than the color of the walls or carpet. Your baby's crib—where the baby will spend many hours alone—must be checked often for small parts and pieces that could present a choking hazard. Make sure the mattress fits snugly, without any gaps, so that the baby can't slip in between the crack and the crib side, and check that crib slots are no more than two and three-eighths inches apart. Lastly, whether you put the crib together yourself or had it put together by the delivery crew, double-check that all screws, bolts, and hardware are in tight to prevent the crib from collapsing.

Be on the safe side and have your home babyproofed by a professional. As your baby grows older, invite your babyproofer back a second and third time, just to make sure that everything is still safe. By creating the safest environment possible, you'll be able to better enjoy every moment spent with your baby at home.

68.

Reconnect with Your Husband

If you're like most mothers, the only time you can find in the day to devote exclusively to your husband is somewhere between one and three in the morning. Unfortunately, he's never awake and ready to chat at that time. Then again, neither are you.

Many couples believe that putting their marriage first means putting their kids second, so they don't do it. But it doesn't have to be that way. When the kids were young, you were probably too tired to go out for a romantic dinner, or too tied to the baby emotionally to leave for a long weekend. But now that your children are a little older, you owe it to yourself and your marriage to get away. Give yourselves the chance to rediscover what made you fall in love in the first place.

Of course there's more to a happy marriage then whisking away for the weekend or having a candlelit dinner for two. A couple needs to develop an appreciation for one another. They need to take time each day to thank each other for small favors. Create rituals that connect you, like making sure you eat dinner together every night, no matter what, or giving each other a kiss every night before bed, even if you've had an argument. These rituals can help your marriage withstand the stresses that often come up.

Through teamwork and communication, and by agreeing to disagree when it comes to parenting, you and your husband can begin to nourish your relationship. It helps to hire that baby-sitter every so often, too, even if it *is* just so that you can talk! Do whatever it takes to give you and your spouse the chance to focus on one another. While parenthood can be exhausting and stressful, under the right conditions, it can also bring a couple closer together. And it can bring a marriage to a level of intimacy that you may never have dreamed possible.

69.

Use Work Skills at Home

There's a reason that you earned the big bucks back when you were working in the nine-to-five world—it's because you were good at what you did! Did you ever think about using those same skills to run your home life? All it takes is incorporating the fundamentals of being a good employee into your parenting repertoire at home.

Any good employee must have great negotiation skills. Such is true with a great mother—have you ever tried to negotiate with a preschooler? In fact, a mother's negotiation skills are probably better-honed than those of the best attorneys in the world. After all, debating with a five-year-old over how long she should be allowed to stay at a friend's house is enough negotiating to last a lifetime.

Star employees are also people who can delegate responsibility. Take a good look at how you manage your home. Are there things your husband, your kids, or your baby-sitter can do so that you don't have to do them? Make a list of everything that needs to get done, and divide up the responsibilities fairly.

Most exemplary employees are terrific problem solvers. Why not teach problem-solving skills to your children? Ask them to come up with solutions to certain situations. For instance, instead of punishing them for constantly fighting with each other, ask them what they think you should do if you catch them fighting. They may offer suggestions that you can really use, such as what they think is acceptable punishment. Chances are that they'll refrain from fighting to avoid their own wrath!

Last, but not least, you should incorporate the most important part of the working world into your home life: the bonus! Your kids deserve a bonus for consistent good behavior. Don't look at this as a bribe, but as a reward. Have your children each decide upon a reasonable reward they would like, should they earn it. Dinner at a favorite restaurant, ice skating lessons, a visit to an arcade — whatever they consider to be most special.

70.
Mothering, 24/7

The hardest part about being a mother is the constant demand that the job makes on your time. Life would be so much easier if we could wake up with our kids at a decent hour, play with them and nurture them all day, and then send them off to bed and relax with a good book. But with children under five at home, it's a good bet that has never happened in your house!

Is it fair? Of course not! Additionally, if you're a mother who works outside of the home, you know that you don't just "knock off" work as soon as you leave the office. You're on your way to your "other" job. Mothering is a twenty-four-hour-a-day job, and just because some moms only work in the home for the final hours of the day doesn't mean that they aren't mothering all day. Working moms know that they are never far from their job of being a mother. Interrupted meetings, days missed because of illness or school functions, and after-school check-in calls all remind us that we are constantly juggling our many responsibilities.

Mothers who work in the home don't have it much easier. They don't change their places of employment, but their hours are just the same.

This all boils down to one premise: Stay healthy! Whether you need a nap or some quiet time to soothe a headache, or you can't breathe because of a massive cold, you are still needed every day, all day. In addition to taking care of their kids, mothers need to make time every day to take care of themselves. Eat properly, stay fit, get as much rest as possible (even a little shut-eye while the baby plays in the crib should do the trick), and keep in mind that mothering is an adventure every day!

71.

C'mon, a Taste Won't Kill You!

The challenge to getting your kids to eat healthy, nutritious foods comes in finding what works best for you and your kids, and then turning buying and eating that good food into an adventure! Whether it's shopping for fresh fruit and vegetables at a farmer's market or creating a delicious new dessert in the kitchen, by exploring different techniques together, you and your family can discover the perfect recipe for healthier eating.

Kids hate to try new foods—especially if they've been told that they're healthy. One way to take the fear out of a new dish is to get your kids involved in its preparation, from buying the ingredients to helping with the cooking. It's a well-known fact that the best way to get your kids to eat is to let them help cook.

True, cooking with kids produces a big mess, and it can take three times the normal cooking time for a simple pizza. But you're going to have to get past the mess and the time frame and just invite them to join you.

There are many tricks to getting your youngsters to prepare and taste new foods. Plan meals around different cultural holidays or choose a color theme for one meal. Prepare the national foods of countries around the world, or use only ingredients that are fresh at that time of year. All these ideas are nutritious *and* educational!

Moms go to all measures to get their kids to eat. Whether your kids enjoy ketchup on everything or will only eat food shaped in squares, their idiosyncrasies will disappear when they are invested in the meal. Sharing the meal preparation with your children is a valuable experience for all involved, and one which they will take well into their youth and adult years.

72.

The Best Birthday Parties Ever

It's easy to head to the nearest indoor playground or arcade for your child's birthday party—they take care of the invitations, the goody bags, and everything in between. All you have to do is show up. Granted, this type of birthday party is a low-stress way to celebrate, but try to get through one of these parties on a budget—it just doesn't happen!

If you aren't in the position to shell out the big bucks for pizza, a slice of cake, and a few arcade games, consider throwing your own birthday party at home or at the nearest park or playground. You don't have to be the most creative mom in town to do so—just the most prepared!

For the four-to seven set, pick a theme that most interests your child—dolls, dinosaurs, pirates, dancing—and plan your party around that theme. For example, a doll party can be as simple as having everyone bring their favorite dolls. Set up all of your daughter's doll paraphernalia and let the guests dress and undress their dolls to their heart's content.

For activities (and this is true for pirates, dinosaurs, or whatever), you can decorate cookies, play games, or do an art project, such as designing T-shirts with iron-ons. For dessert, consider buying a blank cake (ice cream or not) and decorating it yourself. You can buy different edible appliqués just for this purpose, and have your daughter draw her own cake decoration with food coloring and a clean paintbrush. Goody bags can include something theme-oriented and a few pieces of candy.

For older kids, scavenger hunts around your yard or neighborhood are always a fun idea. Or try an arts-and-crafts party with more sophisticated crafts like decoupage, woodworking, or jewelry-making. You can always try kids' favorite—a karaoke party.

All of these parties—even with the T-shirts as giveaways— usually run an average of $200, no matter how many children you invite! Remember to make sure that you have enough adults on hand to help and chaperone. (Ask your parents and siblings, or your baby-sitter.) Limit your party to two hours—you don't want it to drag on.

Most importantly, let your child in on all the planning. Half the fun of doing it yourself is organizing the party and making the decorations and invitations together!

73.

The Mommy Co-op

As soon as you venture forth into public with your infant in tow, it is open season on you. You can count on being bombarded with commentary from other mothers on what you're doing wrong and how to do it right.

Most of the time, this advice turns out to be good advice. And the reason for everyone minding your child-rearing is not mean-spirited. When women go through the various trials and tribulations of mothering, learning what works best and what doesn't, they are often eager to share their newfound information with other mothers in the hopes of making their lives easier.

As a mother, you may want to listen to these other moms' well-intentioned advice. Many times, their tips and suggestions will help things run more smoothly with your baby. Your job is to listen to suggestions, and then analyze them to see if they're worth giving a try. Should a mom you meet at the grocery store tell you not to buy the bottles with the plastic-bag inserts because they tend to leak, consider buying another type of bottle to have on hand should the plastic leak for you. If a different mother on line at the bank tells you not to dress your baby in a heavy bunting to go out because he can overheat, be polite and offer thanks for the suggestion. At home, you and your husband can weigh the pros and cons of using a bunting and make your own decision.

Then think about this: In just a few months, *you're* going to be the mother in the bank, offering unsolicited advice to the new mother you see with *her* baby!

74.

The Stressful Holidays

It's essential that parents work extra hard to play it cool during the holiday season. Of course, when you're rushing about for two months straight, trying to find the perfect gifts, the perfect recipes, the perfect decorations, and the perfect party clothes, it can be easy to lose sight of what the holidays are all about. For this purpose, you may want to incorporate some holiday downtime into your day, every day, beginning November 1.

Set aside an hour of every day when you promise not to be occupied by holiday shopping and cooking concerns. You can use the hour to spend time by yourself or with your children. Use it to find ways of making sure that your kids understand the meaning of the holiday. Read them a story about the origin of your holiday, or discuss with them the emotional aspects of holiday time, such as hope, love, and togetherness.

This holiday season, take time to create new family traditions. It's nice to continue old family traditions with your children during the holidays, but consider starting new ones, as well. Maybe you can visit a soup kitchen on the night before Thanksgiving and make that a yearly thing, or save your Christmas tree decorating for the Saturday night before Christmas.

Create a budget, and stick to it. The biggest source of stress for families occurs when they go overboard on spending. Be realistic about what you can afford to buy. Avoid impulse purchases. To track all of your purchases, use one credit card for all holiday shopping.

Finally, go easy on your kids! Remember that children's tolerance for excitement is much lower than ours. If you dress them in new, uncomfortable clothes, give them unfamiliar food, and stick them with cousins that they haven't seen in years, they're going to be miserable. Let them make some of their own choices during the holidays—about what to wear and what to eat—and they'll be more comfortable and have a better time.

75.

Mothers' Helpers Are a Godsend

A mother's helper is not a baby-sitter. Yes, he or she can sometimes baby-sit if you need to run out, but a mother's helper's primary job function is to give you a hand at home taking care of your children so that you can attend to other things. It will cost you a little, but the relief you'll experience is worth every penny.

The best mother's helper is a young teenager or an older preteen who lives nearby and can walk to your house. In some cases, you may be lucky to find a youngster whose parents will be thrilled that he or she has a place to go every day after school instead of hanging around an empty house! If you can't find a situation such as that, you'll need to pay your mother's helper—but it shouldn't cost you as much per hour as a regular baby-sitter. Bring up the issue of money with your mother's helper before hiring— you may have very different ideas about what fee is reasonable. Discuss this with his or her parents, as well—a case of helping each other out could result in a slightly lower fee for the mother's helper.

Your children will benefit from having a mother's helper, too. If you can leave some of your chores for the latter part of the day when your mother's helper can occupy the children, you'll have more time during the day to spend with the kids. Save cooking, cleaning, and laundry for when the mother's helper is around— then you'll be able to get it all done without interruption, and your kids will have someone to play with in the process.

When hiring a mother's helper, the same rules apply as when hiring a baby-sitter. You'll want to check references or speak to the helper's parents if he or she has not had any previous experience with children. Don't assume that the helper knows how to take care of children—you'll want to give him or her a crash course in baby-sitting, since there may come a time when you need to leave the house.

As with a baby-sitter, give your children proper time to get accustomed to your mother's helper by joining in on their play for the first day or so. Once everybody seems comfortable, you can do other things. Remember that some children with separation anxiety may not like having a mother's helper around while you're still home, and it may take more time for those children to get used to the new situation.

The best part about having a mother's helper is that you can get so many things accomplished. If you're lucky, there will be time left over for you to lock yourself in your room and take a power nap!

76.

Be the "Good Cop" Every So Often

For many mothers—especially those who are the primary caregivers for their kids while their husbands work all week—it's hard to keep from losing their tempers when they're completely frazzled by the end of the day. And what always happens? Just when you lose your cool and start yelling, in walks Daddy, ready to scoop up the kids in his arms and say yes to everything that they've been hounding you for all day. It's called "good cop/bad cop" syndrome, and you've probably seen it done a million times.

On the one hand, you're relieved to have Daddy take over and give you a break. On the other, you feel as though your children are going to grow to resent you, especially when you're the bad cop all of the time.

Many child-rearing experts encourage moms who always have to be the bad parent at home to consider changing their home situations—sometimes drastically. One way to avoid falling into the "bad mommy" rut is to look for an alternative late-day scenario for you and your children. A baby-sitter or a mother's helper in the afternoon can allow for you to be away, and then come home to be on the receiving end of your kids' love and affection. Perhaps a part-time job is something that you should consider. Being away from your kids for a short period regularly may give you a whole new perspective on mothering.

If such a situation isn't possible, you might want to turn to your friends for some help. You may find that some of them feel the same way—always the bad cop while the dads are always the good cop. If this is the case, try swapping childcare twice a week—watch a friend's kid and yours from three to six in the afternoon once, then have your friend take your kids for the same length of time the next day. Why will this work? Simple: It will give you some free time to yourself—and it will give your kids a chance to miss Mommy!

77.

The Wedding Ring Test

Want to know the sex of your baby? Sure, you can ask the doctor to look closely at your sonogram, or wait until you have that amniocentesis, but if you're not headed to the doctor for a few weeks, and you really want to know if it's a boy or girl, you can always perform the wedding ring test. It's simple: Tie your wedding ring onto a piece of string, and then have your husband hold it above your belly while you lie down. If it swings in a circular motion, you're having a girl!

Hopefully, you're quick enough to realize that this gender test is what is more commonly known as a "pregnancy myth." While some common pregnancy myths offer expectant parents an opportunity for a pre-baby giggle or two, others can actually be harmful. Some common myths that are false include the belief that midwives are witches, that a pregnant woman shouldn't raise her arms over her head because the umbilical cord will wrap around her baby's neck, and that a pregnant woman should never take a bath. In truth, most midwives are extremely safe and effective, the movement of a pregnant woman doesn't affect her umbilical cord unless she stands on her head, and a bath is not a dangerous activity for a pregnant woman unless the water temperature is too hot or she slips getting into the tub.

Myth: "If a pregnant woman has indigestion, her baby will have a lot of hair." Millions of completely bald babies are born to mothers who experienced tremendous indigestion during pregnancy!

Myth: "A pregnant woman should lie on her left side during pregnancy." It's true that lying on the left side during pregnancy improves placental and kidney profusion, but if you lie on that side too much, you'll end up with sores! The bottom line is that a woman should lie in whatever position is comfortable for her.

It is a good idea for you to become familiar with such myths so that you do not do anything harmful to your health or the health of the baby. As for the wedding ring test, by all means, have some fun! But it's probably not a good idea to decorate your nursery based on the results!

78.

Teach the Meaning of Respect

Unless you teach children why manners are important, they won't really learn them. First, they must learn about being considerate, courteous, and kind—concepts toddlers can understand—to realize that others have feelings that are similar to their own.

Lay the foundation for teaching your children respect at home before expecting them to show respect in the outside world. Start with discussing "the Golden Rule" with your children: Treat others as you would have them treat you. It's also a good idea to explain that the Golden Rule also means being nice to somebody so that they'll be nice to you in return.

In addition, you're going to need to practice what you preach, and this means remembering your manners all of the time. Show your children what it's like to be nice and friendly to others and to say "please" and "thank you" whenever the situation calls for it. Include these words when you're speaking to your kids, as well as,

"I'm sorry," "excuse me," and "you're welcome." Be sure to praise your kids every time they use these terms.

Above all, your children should learn to be considerate of themselves. Teach them that it's perfectly acceptable to tell someone what they don't like or want ("No thank you; I don't like grape juice") or to stand up for themselves if other children try to take advantage of them ("You can use my ball when I'm finished with it").

The benefits of teaching your children respect and social graces are tremendous. You'll not only do your share to make the world a nicer, more courteous place, but you'll boost your children's self-confidence. Just don't expect them to learn perfect manners overnight—it can take years for children to think beyond their own needs and become respectful and considerate people.

79.

Sweet September

It's not that we don't love our kids, but having them around all summer—often complaining of boredom—can be aggravating for even the most hands-on, active parents. We try to fill their summers with activities and fun, but there are always days—sometimes weeks—where there's nothing to do. Or sometimes, we overload them with activities to keep from being bored and they become frazzled. Though many kids complain about having to go back to school in September, they're probably secretly glad to have something different to do!

Still, the transition from summer vacation to school can be very unsettling for a child of any age. It's important for parents to start putting their kids at ease, about a week or so before the first day of school.

For a younger child, pay a visit to her school a few days before it opens (the teachers will be there, preparing for opening day) and visit the classroom. Your child may even get the chance to meet her teacher, if she hasn't already.

Talk to your child about what to expect at school. Go through her day as best you can—where she'll eat lunch, the place where she'll line up for the bus, and where the bathrooms are. Answer all of her questions so that she'll feel more confident about the whole thing.

Get your child to bed early, starting a full week before the first day. Summers are filled with opportunities to stay up late, and your child may have already fallen into a routine that includes a later bedtime. Push bedtime up one hour and work it from there.

Finally, express your joy! Make the first day back a great one for you, too! Invite some other mothers over for breakfast to talk about school, your kids' teachers, or what you're going to do with your newfound freedom. Then begin preparing yourself for three o'clock, when the kids come home again.

80.

Color-Code Your Kids

This chapter mostly applies to mothers of two or more children. With one child, after-school activities are pretty easy to keep track of. But toss one or two more active kids into the mix, and you've got to work that much harder just to keep it all together!

Before your after-school and weekend children's activities start for the year, visit your local office supply store and buy a really big dry-erase board. Look for one with a blank calendar on top and a lot of extra space on bottom. At home, choose a space to put your board. The kitchen is the best place, but keep it out of reach, because little hands can accidentally rub off important information.

Indulge in a pack of multicolored dry-erase markers. The most organized way to create your schedule is to use different colored markers for each child. You'll also need an additional color for your activities, and still another for your husband's.

Begin by numbering the calendar boxes, writing in the appropriate month and year and the days of the week. Then fill in your activities first—business trips, hair appointments, doctor visits—and next, your husband's.

Now, it's time to schedule your kids. In the empty space below the calendar, list the days of the week and give each its own column. Then, beginning with the Monday column, use each specific color to write in each child's activity for that day, including the time and location. Using the same color, make a large colored dot for each activity in every Monday box on the calendar. For example, if your son has piano lessons and soccer practice on Monday, and his color is green, put two green dots in every Monday on the calendar, and write out the specifics for both those activities in the Monday column below. Continue on through the week, and then do the exact same thing for each child.

Will you look like a lunatic mother with this in your kitchen? Will other mothers laugh at you and call you obsessive? Perhaps. But *you'll* be the one laughing in the end—all the way to the soccer field, and the dance studio, and the pool.

81.

Choosing a Pediatrician

Whatʼs the best way to go about picking the right doctor for your family? Do you opt for the doctor thatʼs closest to your house, or do you use the same group of pediatricians that your neighbor swears by?

The first step is to pay both of these offices a visit. Choosing a pediatrician is not something to be taken lightly. Schedule an "interview" visit with the doctors recommended to you — keep it to no more than three. Never solely trust someoneʼs recommendation — meet with the doctor first to see if he or she is right for your family. If you need to get possible doctorsʼ names, the best sources are your obstetrician, another doctor you trust, or your childʼs principal or nursery school director.

After your visit, donʼt make the mistake of forgetting to check the doctorʼs credentials. Find out whether he or she is board-certified in pediatrics and how much experience the doctor has. A highly qualified doctor will generally give you better referrals to specialists when needed. Also, check the doctor's hospital affiliation—should your children ever need hospitalization, you'll want to make sure that they're going to be well cared for in a comfortable, efficient facility.

Ask questions! By asking a lot of questions during your interview, you'll learn more about the practice and the inner workings of the office. Are there walk-in hours? Saturday hours? Who schedules checkups? What happens if your doctor is not available in an emergency? And most important, how does the office handle late-night phone calls?

Give the doctor and yourself a chance to get comfortable with one another. A personality fit is important, but it's not the most important thing when it comes to medical care. Not every fantastic pediatrician has the best bedside manner. First, choose a doctor that you feel will give your children the best care ever—then take some time getting used to his or her personality. If you still aren't happy after a few visits, start at the beginning again and find a new doctor.

82.

A Vacation *Can* Be Relaxing!

Recently, a number of vacation spots offering children's activities, communal dining, childcare, and extra-large lounge areas where guests can mingle began popping up all over. Parents can now have a lot of family time with family-oriented activities, and also spend time alone while their children enjoy a kid's club or camp. Some hotels even provide childcare at night so that adults can be by themselves.

Check into whether your hotel or resort has screened their baby-sitters and made sure that they know how to care for children. Many hotels offer extensive baby-sitting training courses which their employees are urged to repeat several times during the year. Find out if the resort that you choose for your vacation trains their camp directors, counselors, and baby-sitters.

Moms and dads need time away from their kids to wind down and re-energize. You're paying for your kids' vacation, you're offering them an array of exciting activities, and you're feeding and entertaining them. They're having fun! You should be, too.

83.

Learn to Be Heavier

You may have spent your whole life trying to make the scale needle move to the left. You've passed up on cake at parties and dessert at dinner, and you've finally learned to combat those afternoon snack attacks.

Pregnancy, however, is not the time to be dieting! Dieting while pregnant puts your baby at risk of losing nutrients, and extreme dieting can release toxic substances that may harm the fetus. This doesn't mean that pregnancy is an excuse to gorge on cake and scarf down chips. You're supposed to gain weight during pregnancy, but you're supposed to gain healthy weight—not too much weight. Too much weight is bad for you and your baby, and will be extremely difficult to lose after your baby is born.

It's strange to step on the scale during your first pregnancy and watch yourself gain, in some cases, a lot of weight. As the numbers go up, so may your anxieties: "Am I gaining too much?" "Will I be able to lose the weight after the baby comes?" Try not to get caught up in stressing over your weight gain during pregnancy. If watching the scale becomes a great source of anxiety, try ditching it completely. Hide it in the basement, or ask a friend to keep it at her house for the duration of your pregnancy. You'll be weighed at your monthly or weekly doctor visits anyway.

So how much weight *should* you gain during pregnancy? Discuss your weight with your obstetrician. Stay within the guidelines for pregnancy weight gain. Your optimal gain depends on your pregnancy body mass, based on weight and height. Experts agree that steady weight gain throughout your pregnancy is ideal. The way to achieve that is to make smart choices and keep healthy foods available at home. Stay away from rich, fatty foods when you can.

Learn to love the way you look with your new big belly. Relish your full-figured reflection—naked or clothed. You'll be astonished at what a woman's body can achieve!

84.

Mothering Other People's Kids

It happens to every mother—she finds herself in the position of having to discipline somebody else's child. It might be the little boy on the playground who insists on climbing up the slide while her daughter is trying to slide down, or the little girl in her son's kindergarten class that punches him in the arm every day after school. There will come a time when you have to step in and take some action.

It's a tricky situation for many reasons. Do you let your child work these things out on his own? Do you find the other child's parents and ask them to handle the situation? Or do you reprimand the other child yourself and ask her to play somewhere else?

The truth is that all three of these solutions are correct in certain situations. Your child *can* work things out on his own, provided that he isn't hurt, and sometimes it may be best to let him. If your child is crying, you may want to approach both children and explain how to behave. Just having an authoritative figure spell out the rules may be all that a child needs to change her behavior.

If that fails, you could involve the offender's parent or caregiver. Just be forewarned—some parents take offense when someone suggests that their child is misbehaving. Speak to the parent in a friendly manner: "I never know what to do in these situations—any ideas?" This focuses on solving the problem rather than blaming the child and putting the other parent on the defensive.

When play is at your home, you have the advantage when it comes to enforcing the rules. Basically, whatever you say goes! When your child has new playmates come over for the first time, make sure you explain the house rules to them. Be sure to be clear and firm about the rules, and point out that they may differ from the rules in their houses. And should a rule be defied? First, reinforce the rule and give a warning. If the misconduct still occurs, gently remove the child from the situation, and offer both children another activity. If all else fails, you might want to call the child's parents. But again, choose your words carefully!

Refrain from yelling at other children—just as you refrain from yelling at your own kids—no matter how horribly they're misbehaving. In most cases, it's good to ask yourself what you'd want another parent to do if your child were behaving in an unfavorable manner.

85.

Mommies Have Friends, Too

When a woman becomes a mother, she needs friends more than ever, but she also has less time for them—that's the unpleasant reality. If you find yourself in this situation, you need to do everything in your power to maintain your best circle of friends. Connect frequently—by e-mail or on the telephone—and schedule a girls' night out every couple of months. Treat the date as important—no matter how exhausted you are, go anyway.

For most women, having a child also inspires the need to forge new bonds with other mothers who share similar experiences. They often seek out other mothers with children the same age because it makes sense to gravitate toward other women who have similar things in common. Such friendships often last for years.

It's important for a mother to socialize with these new friends without the children around, too. It's incredible what new things you can learn about a woman who you've seen at the playground every day for a year in just one evening over coffee!

86.

Solutions to Back-Talk

When children begin flexing their linguistic muscles, it can be quite alarming for parents. At first, it can be sort of cute, but as children get older and their vocabulary expands, you may be left with otherwise angelic children saying things like "Duh, you idiot!" and "Dumb stupid head." This behavior isn't cute and silly anymore; it's rude and disrespectful. It is a parent's responsibility to teach children how to express themselves in ways that are respectful.

When kindergartners and first graders mouth off, it's almost always with words that they learned from television or on the playground at school. They don't necessarily mean to hurt feelings with their words—they're just imitating their friends. Don't take it to heart if your daughter calls you a "blubber-butt." She's probably just repeating a phrase that she heard elsewhere—one that she hoped you might find funny or silly.

Getting angry and punishing a young offender is a common mistake that parents make—one that only fuels the child's anger.

Instead, try responding to the rudeness by saying, "That's hurtful," or "Please don't talk with mean words." Add a clear warning about the consequences of using that language again. If discipline becomes necessary, you may want to take away a privilege—it should be something that you can follow through with.

Older kids mouth off for different reasons. They've learned how to use words for maximum impact! They have a better understanding of other people's feelings, and mouthing off is their way to assert independence. If your child's expressions are starting to get out of hand, let the least offensive words go without comment (don't call attention to them), and let the more disrespectful phrases like "Shut up" garner a punishment.

Finally, if your youngsters continue to speak in an offensive way, you may want to consider policing what they're watching on television. Even "harmless" cartoon shows can glamorize disrespectful phrases.

87.

"Leave Me Alone!"

Teen angst (or preteen angst) comes along very suddenly. It's enough to scare any mother into rushing to the first child psychologist that she can find. According to child development experts, the pressure for today's kids to take on grown-up responsibilities and overloaded schedules often pushes them into acting moody well before they reach thirteen.

If the signs are there—your child appears withdrawn, aloof, angry, or secretive—this behavior, though alarming, is actually healthy. Experts say that it's an indication that he has the confidence to separate from his parents. If, in addition to these signs, however, your child experiences loss of appetite, can't sleep, or shows other signs of distress for an extended period of time, it may indicate a more serious problem like depression. In that case, talk to your child's doctor.

There are steps you can take to make both your lives easier. One of these is to take a step back. It's important not to overreact or draw extra attention to your child's rebelliousness. He may seem to dislike you, or even complain to his friends that you don't understand him, but it's doubtful that he really feels this way. He may need to feel irritated by you in order for him to move ahead.

Try relating to him on his level. That doesn't mean taking an interest in the latest heavy metal band that he likes or dressing like a teenager to make him think that you're cool. Help him see that you, too, passed through those awkward years.

Be a little flexible when it comes to your rules and regulations. You want your child to know that you acknowledge that he's growing up. Continue to provide him with structure and guidance, but make certain exceptions, like moving his bedtime later, or letting him miss a soccer practice when he just doesn't feel like going. You'll be giving him the space he needs, which may result in him being less resentful of your authority in his life.

88.

Sleep-Away Camp

At first, it sounds like a truly wonderful idea—your nine-year-old has asked to go to sleep-away camp for a month with her friends this summer. You have visions of stretching out on a lounge chair next to your partner on summer evenings while your daughter plays endless games under the guidance and supervision of a mature camp staff. What could be better? Sleep-away camp offers kids refuge from the pressures of home and school. It's a place where children can renew their sense of being kids and enhance their self-reliance, cooperation, and independence.

But before you fork over the exorbitant fee for summer camp, you need to be sure that your child is ready for an extended away-from-home adventure. Does she become worried or agitated at the mere mention of camp, or is she pulling her duffel bag out from under the bed, getting it ready even though it's only April? If the first is true, you may want to skip the trip this summer and wait for next year.

You also need to take into consideration how well your child interacts with other children and adult authority figures. If she's able to make friends easily and has no problems accepting authority, she's probably ready. It helps if your child has been away before—maybe slept away at her grandparents' or a friend's house once or twice without incident.

As for *your* readiness—truth be told, the day that your child first leaves for camp is incredibly difficult. You can expect a teary good-bye (on your part), but rest assured, most of the time, children make new friends almost immediately on the bus.

After a few days, it gets better. You'll begin to relax—one perk about camp is that you know where your child is at all times and don't need to worry. By the end of the first week, after you've sent her enough mail to cover the entire month, you'll actually begin to forget her for extended periods of time. By week two, your letters will get shorter, and by the third week, you'll be counting the few weeks you have left for yourself.

89.
Worrying, 24/7

Mothers spend a lot of time worrying about their children—and with just cause. When young children are involved, there are thousands of valid reasons to worry, including all of those safety issues. You may wonder if there will ever be a time in your life as a mother when you can just sit back and relax.

Unfortunately, there won't be! In fact, mothers (and fathers) worry about their children from the moment that they're born until well into the children's adult lives!

When children reach middle school or junior high, parents worry that they won't fit in, make friends, or be popular. There's nothing more heartbreaking to parents than to see their child with low self-esteem or feeling left out of the crowd. As we parents look on from the sidelines, it can pain us to see our children mistreated by their peers.

From the time that they are babies, we try to boost our children's self-esteem. Then some bully comes along and suddenly, your child feels like an outcast. What can a mother do? You can talk through your children's experiences and help them to see themselves in a more balanced way. You can listen to them and validate their feelings. Don't dismiss your child's complaints that he "doesn't have any friends" or that "everyone picks on him." That will only make him feel more isolated and misunderstood.

Regardless of where your child falls on the popularity scale, it's up to you to facilitate healthy friendships. Having just one good friend helps to buffer the negative effects of not being popular. Take your child and his friend out bowling on the weekends, or to a video arcade or ballgame. The loving support from parents and one really good buddy are all he'll need to survive in the kid-eat-kid world of schoolyard popularity.

We can't protect our children from all the hurt that they will endure in their social lives. However, we can certainly help them to adapt to their circumstances and share the tough lessons that we learned about life back when we were on the playground.

90.

Homework Survival

The single biggest source of frustration in many households is homework. With all of kids' extracurricular activities, and the array of subjects assigned each night, they have a difficult time buckling down and getting the work done. For many kids, the overload of activities plus schoolwork leaves them no time for themselves.

In the early elementary years, homework can instill good study habits and dispel the notion that learning only occurs in school. As children advance through middle school and beyond, the link between doing homework and getting good grades strengthens. But parents these days find themselves questioning the role of homework: What should kids get out of it? What makes a good assignment? How much should I help? And, furthermore, how much is too much?

Homework challenges our kids with an opportunity to practice what they're learning in school. As their cognitive abilities increase, kids can handle tougher, lengthier assignments. For children of all ages, a parent's job is to help them balance the load. The National PTA recommends no more than twenty minutes of homework per school day for kids in kindergarten through second grade, and thirty to sixty minutes per day for kids in third through sixth. However, schools and teachers across the country vary on how much homework they give students.

Set a routine for your child. A regularly scheduled time every day will help her learn to motivate herself each day. Teachers recommend that your child does homework as soon as she comes home from school, after a light snack. Select a location for homework, too — a quiet spot free of distractions. Remain available to answer questions — perhaps join your child at the table while she does her homework, and pay bills or do other paperwork.

The greatest benefit of homework is that it encourages a child to be an independent thinker. For this reason alone, parents should be cautious about how much help they give their child. Remember that your child is responsible for completing her assignment. As tempting as it may be for you to take over, support her instead by helping her find an answer, or showing her how to work through a problem. Never do her work for her — this defeats the purpose of homework.

91.

Kids on Board, Not Bored

For many parents, the thought of a road trip with the family conjures up more stress and anxiety than the idea of bungee jumping into the Grand Canyon. The constant bickering and rest-stopping is enough to make any driver lose control. But it doesn't have to be that way. With enough foresight and planning, a family road trip can be the best way for families to spend time together, see the country, and experience new, exciting things.

Before you set foot in the minivan, your route should be mapped out to avoid any unpleasant surprises. Choose routes that take you through interesting places with sights to explore along the way. Get a map to find museums, historical landmarks, and restaurants that you wouldn't ordinarily know about. Provide your kids with maps of their own, so that they can track their journey, as well. Ask your children to circle three places that they would like to see along your route—that way, they have something to look forward to and feel more involved in the trip.

The key to pleasant travel time is a well-stocked vehicle. Snacks, beverages, CDs, travel games, books—anything that you think will occupy your children during the less interesting legs of your trip. The all-time best road trip idea is to listen to books on tape or CD. Choose stories that the whole family will enjoy.

Before leaving, allow each of your kids to pack a car bag—a backpack filled with their favorite things to do. Let them bring markers and paper, body-art pencils, handheld video games—whatever will hold their interest when there's nothing to see out the window.

Separate squabbles with a cooler placed strategically on the seat in between your kids. This will provide them with easy access to the snacks they love, and act as a divider for preventing the inevitable quarreling.

When all else fails, you can always rely on the classic car games. Try the license-plate game (find as many states as you can, or find the letters of the alphabet in order); the geography game (name a place; the next person must then use the last letter in the place name as the first letter in the name of another place); and Twenty Questions (someone thinks of a person or thing and everyone else asks twenty yes-or-no questions before guessing who or what it is).

Above all, remember to stop every so often to let your kids blow off some steam. Rest-stop playgrounds or fast-food restaurants with indoor play areas are your best bet, but your kids will *really* love you if you call it quits early every day and hit the motel pool!

92.

Organizing Your Minivan

Not to imply that every mom should have a minivan. It's just that in this day and age, for a less stressful experience driving children around town, many parents opt for a minivan for the extra room and comfort it provides.

Still, no matter what type of family car you own—minivan, truck, or sedan—keeping it organized and clean is the only way that you can survive suburban life in your automobile. Moms spend countless hours driving and carpooling, and things can get pretty hairy if you can't easily find change for the tolls, the baby's extra pacifier, your bottled water, or a favorite CD.

Organize your vehicle the way that you would organize your home. Have plenty of trash receptacles, a good supply of snacks and bottled water, and a bag filled with fun things for your kids to do should they be detained in the car for any reason. Don't forget to include doubles of items that your children absolutely can't go without: pacifiers, blankets, extra AA batteries (for handheld games or CD players), and baby wipes.

Of course, it's important to have a first-aid kit in your car, complete with bandages, gauze pads, cotton, antibiotic cream, and surgical tape. Keep it in your trunk, along with a blanket, jumper cables, a jack, a spare tire, flares, a box of matches, and a jug of water. It always helps to be prepared for any situation.

Make good use of your glove compartment—many people overstuff theirs, rendering it useless in an emergency. Don't keep road maps in there—many cars and minivans offer door storage shelves for maps. Limit your glove compartment to your car instruction manual, registration papers, a flashlight, and a bottle of acetaminophen. (You'll need it sooner or later.)

The most important items to have in your car are snacks! It never fails—as soon as you find yourself stuck in traffic, your children will either have to go to the bathroom or find themselves "starving to death." You may not be able to get to a restroom so easily, but you can at least offer the kids a bite to take their minds off of their full bladders!

93.

Make a Date with Your Kids!

Family nights are an occasion for family members to pay attention to each other. The challenge lies in picking the perfect night for family night, and sticking to it, no matter how busy your schedules get! Rituals give kids a sense of security, because they know that they belong to something special. So once you pick your night, make it happen every week.

Sunday is really the perfect night for family night. On Sunday night, most families do nothing—they just wind down from a busy weekend. But Sunday evenings are also usually free of social engagements, kids' activities, or meetings. It's a pivotal time to regroup as a family.

Once your family night has been established, people in the family should take turns to pick the activity for the night. This way, everyone gets a turn. Kids will begin to resent family night if the parents always dictate what to do.

Consider making an occasional break from traditional family pastimes like board games or watching videos. Instead, hop in the car and visit your local bookstore. It will probably have a variety of kids' books, and often, a pretty good cappuccino for Mom and Dad to enjoy.

Another fun idea is to turn your kitchen into a restaurant. Plan the menu for Sunday night dinner together, and give each person a list of what they should do to prepare for the meal. Share the cooking, set the table with the best china, get dressed up, and dine as if you were royalty!

Another off-the-wall suggestion is to have a family talent show. Announce this one week ahead of time so that you can all prepare for your performances. Sing, dance, tell jokes — you may learn that your kids have talents you never knew about.

The jigsaw puzzle is an oldie but a goodie for a good reason. It builds family togetherness, and the quiet time allows for families to engage in conversation.

Not to say that there isn't something wonderful about playing a good old board game or watching a great family flick together. Keep in mind that the most important part of family night — no matter what night you choose to have it — is spending uninterrupted time with your husband and kids, free from distractions. It can be a family tradition that your children will pass down to their children.

94.

Making Memorable Moments

On your next family vacation, resist the urge to stop in the souvenir shop for store-bought trinkets. Instead, create your own collection of vacation remembrances that will be much more meaningful to your family in the years to come.

"Free" souvenirs can be found at just about every vacation spot in the world, if only you search for them. At the beach, for instance, if your kids are like all other kids, they'll insist on collecting a bucket full of shells. Next time you're vacationing at the shore, ask your children to limit their collection to five "great" shells. Then collect some sand in a plastic bag and bring it home with the shells to make a terrarium in a glass jar. Decorate a colorful label, and include the name of the beach and the date that you were there, and you have yourself a wonderful, homemade souvenir.

For creating other interesting, handmade souvenirs, pay a visit to the nearest tourist information center and collect every brochure, map, or program that they provide for free. Back at home (or at the hotel), have your children cut and glue different pictures from the brochures on a piece of construction paper. You can later have the entire thing laminated for use as a place mat.

For a nominal fee, postcards of your vacation spot are almost always available at the local drugstore or at your hotel. Have your kids write the postcards to themselves and mail them home each day of your trip. You'll probably arrive home before the postcards do, but your kids will enjoy reading their vacation thoughts and reminiscing over the fun times they had.

There are many creative ways to preserve vacation memories. The problem is that most parents think of them when it's too late. Prepare for your next vacation ahead of time by bringing along paints, markers, sequins, glue, and other small arts-and-crafts supplies. Remember to take along a plastic box for storing your children's artwork during the trip. Years later, these souvenirs will be a lot more meaningful to look at than a silly snow globe or back-scratcher that says, "I visited Miami Beach!"

95.

Appreciate Your Family Every Day

If it seems that things typically get out of hand in your home—where the discipline and time-outs are suddenly outweighing the fun and joy, it's time to make some changes. It's time to learn how to experience joy with your family once again.

How do happy families do it? They follow principles that increase the joy in their relationships. There's no secret formula to these principles—the families just practice habits that ultimately increase the joy in their lives. They take time during the day to appreciate the little things that make their children laugh—dancing around the house with a towel around your head, building towers just to knock them down, or carrying an armful of pillows and dropping them. Mothers need to grab these opportunities whenever possible—even if it means that you'll be late for something.

It's a common misconception that happy families are the popular ones that are invited to every neighborhood cookout, or the ones rushing off to see every street fair or museum within a ten-mile radius. But some of the happiest childhood memories are often created right in a family's own backyard: kids squirting Mom and Dad with a hose; bird-watching in the early hours of the morning; gardening together.

Happy families include as many rituals as possible into their lives. Perhaps they eat out every Sunday night together or go for a walk together every evening after dinner. Predictability and regularity are the key. Children feel most comfortable when they know what to expect. That's not to say a little unexpected surprise every now and then won't delight your youngsters! Go for a walk in pajamas or take a drive just before bedtime—some of the best family times come as a result of breaking from the norm and doing the unexpected.

Often, the most memorable moments your child will have will consist of activities that are fun for him, while to you, they probably seem boring. Mopping the floor, for example, can be a three-year-old's happiest activity—what's more fun than playing in soapy water? Turn your household work into playtime fun for you and your children—hand-wash dishes together, vacuum, or get them to help you wash the car or the dog.

These chores will probably take double the time with children involved. The jobs may not be finished quite to your satisfaction, but you're going to need to stop watching the clock and valuing efficiency, and start thinking of these tasks as valuable opportunities for some major family fun!

96.
Turn It Off!

Chances are that if you have children, they're watching between three and four hours of television a day. Now, television is not all bad—there are many educational, entertaining programs for children. But consider this: Studies show that a lot of television can make children less social. It can also lead to weight gain, shorten their attention span, and make it harder for them to learn how to read, analyze, and solve problems. This can then lead to lower grades and low self-esteem. For these reasons, it's essential that you become the boss of the television in your house and begin setting limits for your kids.

Limit the time per week that you allow your child to watch. For children under five, it's reasonable to let them watch TV for one hour a day—often that means two programs. Though the American Academy of Pediatrics recommends that children under two not watch any TV, that may be a difficult rule to enforce, especially if there are older siblings at home.

Next, sit down with your child and help him select the two programs he's going to watch and the time that he's going to watch them. Limit him to children's networks only—but make sure that you're familiar with the programs he selects. Just because they are on children's networks doesn't mean that the program will be wholesome and violence-free.

Once you've chosen his two shows, watch them with him! Ask your child about what he believes the true consequences might be of some of the actions he may witness on TV. Take advantage of such "teachable moments" every way possible. Studies show that kids mimic the behavior that they see on TV. Since a young child doesn't necessarily understand the consequences of those actions in the real world, certain situations displayed on TV need to be discussed.

Most important, don't turn off the TV without providing your children with alternative activities. As soon as that power button is turned off, you're going to be met with plenty of protest. Beat them to the punch by keeping plenty of arts-and-crafts materials, stacks of books, and outdoor toys and sports equipment on hand. Consider enrolling your child in art or music classes. Or hop in the car and visit the library—anything to get him away from the tube. The bookstore, a children's museum, even the mall—all are good places to take your kids when they begin to show signs of cartoon withdrawal.

97.

Quick Boost: Saying "I Love You"

In addition to the kisses and hugs that we shower our children with, there are many ways to tell them, "I love you." Whether it's with a secret wink or gesture, or shouting it through a megaphone, it's important for parents to find different ways to communicate their love to their children.

A good example is the mothers who leave notes for their kids around the house where their children will see them during the course of their mornings. These are sweet and simple messages that say "I love you," or clever pictures for children who can't yet read.

Another way for mother and child to communicate is to use sign language. Look for books on sign language at your local library. Then teach your child the simple signs for "I love you" or "Great job!" and experience the joy of sharing a "secret" language with your child!

Some mothers leave notes or small treats in their children's lunchboxes for them to find during school. Other moms mail letters of love to their kids. Still others—especially working moms—call their children just to let them know that they're thinking of them.

Look for creative ways to tell your children that you love them. Frame photographs of you together, and write personal messages of love on the backs. Look through photo albums together of your children as babies, and tell them about the funny things that they did that made you and their father laugh. Keep a record of all of the funny moments in your house throughout the year, and then read them over on her birthday. Or take each child away for a day or weekend—just the two of you—for some special mother/daughter or mother/son bonding time.

When it comes to saying, "I love you," you should never wait for a special occasion, or even nightfall, to tell your child. Anytime is a good time for kisses and hugs. You know how they make *you* feel—think of how great they will feel to your child!

98.

Becoming a Nine-to-Fiver Again

If the thought of returning to work again terrifies you, rest assured that millions of moms across the country make it out the door every morning. What you need to do is to focus on a morning routine filled with shortcuts and secrets to getting it all together. Here are a few simple tricks to make life easier for mothers who are about to re-enter the nine-to-five world.

The first rule for working mothers is to adjust to wearing less makeup! This can shave precious minutes off your morning regimen. Before you go back to work, visit your favorite department store makeup counter, and ask the salesperson for some advice on shortening your makeup routine.

Consider getting a short, easy-to-manage haircut. A cropped style looks great and is low-maintenance in the morning. For some extra, worthwhile pampering, treat yourself to having your eyebrows shaped at your salon the day before you return to work. Makeup experts say that this procedure brightens your eyes and opens your face, resulting in a more polished look.

The most important part of your morning routine is setting aside time for your children. Whether it is with some pre-shower, still-in-bed cuddles or eating breakfast together, it's vital that you give them some of your undivided attention before leaving.

If possible, return to work on a Friday and treat it as a dress rehearsal. Check out what your coworkers are wearing, and then you can go clothes shopping over the weekend.

There's no question that returning to work after maternity leave—or after five years of mothering at home—is stressful. Just remember not to be too hard on yourself. New mothers put pressure on themselves at work to pretend that everything is the same as it was before they had kids. They'll pretend that they're not exhausted most of the time as a result of taking care of children, and that their focus is completely on the job. With kids at home or school while you're at work, it may be easier to complete your tasks, but you can bet that you'll be thinking of them and wondering what they're doing all day long.

99.

Take Pride in Your Mothering

Every mother gains a certain amount of perspective and insight into raising children after she's been doing it for a while. But no matter how long you've been mothering, you'll still meet with that gnawing feeling from time to time that makes you think that you're not handling certain situations correctly. No parent has all of the answers all of the time, but by following some simple parenting guidelines, you'll be able to give yourself a pat on the back for being a successful mom.

Obviously, the best thing that you can do for your kids is provide them with unconditional love and encouragement. Listen to them when they talk, and show them that you value them and acknowledge their feelings. Support them and foster self-approval, making them less reliant on the acceptance of others.

Your children should be your highest priority. Despite the enormous demands that life takes on our time and energy, learn to distinguish the important things like spending time with your kids, playing with them, and teaching them right from wrong.

Consistent discipline is the best way to help your child learn the rules. Set clear limits, and enforce them consistently. When your children break the rules, respond in ways that won't hurt their self-esteem—a warning or scolding for minor infractions; a time-out for larger offenses; and logical consequences each time. As long as you're consistent, your child will learn from every situation.

Chronic sleep deprivation, isolation, and self-neglect can leave a mother physically depleted, emotionally discouraged, and, ultimately, ineffective. Take time to renew your perspective, enthusiasm, sense of humor, and energy. Do whatever it takes to promote your own well-being—a night out with friends, an evening watching a good movie, or just some time in the day for deep breathing exercises. Never deny yourself time to regroup—just a little time alone may be all that you need. You'll be better able to take care of your children because you will have taken care of yourself.

If you teach your children to be responsible, they'll learn how to look for solutions on their own when they face setbacks or failures. Help them understand that they are responsible for the choices that they make, as well as the consequences of their actions. If you go out of your way to teach your children how to be kind, respectful, and courteous, you can call yourself a successful mother!

100.

Mother's Day

You watch them as they play hide-and-seek in the backyard and your heart fills with joy. You peek in on them as they sleep peacefully in their beds at night and you're filled with emotion. You relish every milestone—first steps, first teeth, and first days of school—with enormous pride and tremendous love and gratitude. Though you may have shuddered at the thought of it before they were born, you suddenly realize that your children have taken over your life—and you couldn't be happier!

The intensity of our love for our children is sometimes too much to bear. For most mothers, the love that they have for their children is an unexplainable amount of love—yet the power of it is sometimes frightening, this capacity to love *so much*. It makes us wonder: Did we always have the capacity to love like this, or is it something our children have conjured up in us?

Being responsible for our children's health and happiness gives us a greater purpose in life than ever before. The next time your daughter whispers, "I love you, Mommy," or your son makes a napkin holder especially for you in preschool, ask yourself this question:

Is there anything in life more rewarding than being a mother?